LIVING OFF CRIME

LIVING OFF CRIME

Second Edition

KENNETH D. TUNNELL

ROWMAN & LITTLEFIELD PUBLISHERS, INC.
Lanham • Boulder • New York • Toronto • Oxford

ROWMAN & LITTLEFIELD PUBLISHERS, INC.

Published in the United States of America
by Rowman & Littlefield Publishers, Inc.
A wholly owned subsidiary of The Rowman & Littlefield Publishing Group, Inc.
4501 Forbes Boulevard, Suite 200, Lanham, Maryland 20706
www.rowmanlittlefield.com

PO Box 317
Oxford
OX2 9RU, UK

British Library Cataloguing in Publication Information Available

Library of Congress Cataloging-in-Publication Data

Tunnell, Kenneth D.
  Living off crime / Kenneth D. Tunnell.—2nd ed.
      p. cm.
  Includes bibliographical references and index.
  ISBN 0-7425-4196-7 (cloth : alk. paper)—ISBN 0-7425-4197-5 (pbk. : alk.
paper)
  1. Thieves. 2. Criminal behavior. 3. Crime—Social aspects. 4. Social classes.
I. Title.

  HV6648.T86 2006
  364.3'73—dc22   2005017288

Printed in the United States of America

♾™ The paper used in this publication meets the minimum requirements of
American National Standard for Information Sciences—Permanence of Paper for
Printed Library Materials, ANSI/NISO Z39.48-1992.

CONTENTS

ACKNOWLEDGMENTS

There are few academic activities quite as humbling or exciting as writing. It is an arduous task that at some point demands one's proclamation that "It is finished." Yet, as many people realize far better than I do, books never possess the final word. This one is no exception.

Mine is a book with a bias, for it is designed to bring class back into discussions of the contemporary predatory crime problem. From time to time, social class becomes less central to the sociological lexicon. This book argues, though, that social class is fundamental to shared ways of life, culture, and consciousness. Social class, as shown in this book, remains relevant to the group of street criminals that frequently and actively engages in disproportionate numbers of property crime. Beyond that, the book relates class to this group's subcultures and consciousness, shaped by (among other things) social structure, life chances, routine criminal activities, and a street-centered existence. Although street criminals' consciousness little resembles orthodox explications of class-infused action or praxis, consciousness, as mediated through life-shaping structures and actions, is relevant to their sustained criminality and daily lifestyles.

I owe a tremendous gratitude to numerous individuals for their ongoing support. Thanks goes especially to Lance Selva and Bruce Mallard and the late Frank Lee for pointing the way and setting the course; to Jeff Ferrell and Mark Hamm for friendship and inspiration; to graduate assistant Ryan Bussard for his invaluable help with this second edition; to the anonymous reviewers for their insightful criticisms and recommendations; to Ron Akers, Gregg Barak, Jim Black, Bob Bohm, Vic Bumphus, Don Clelland, Terry Cox, Walter DeKeseredy, John Denton, Carole Garrison, Keith Hayward, Mike Presdee, Jeffrey Ian Ross, Bankole Thompson, Sam

Wallace, and Barbara Warner for their friendship, support, and ongoing interest in my work.

Alan McClare at Rowman & Littlefield first approached me about writing this second edition. Alan's encouragement and combined enthusiasm and patience helped bring this edition along to completion.

Thanks, yet again, to Ilona.

1

CRIME AND CRIMINALS

Research of the past three decades reveals that a small group of adult males is responsible for a disproportionate amount (perhaps as much as 60 percent) of all serious property crimes such as burglary and robbery. This group, which is believed to comprise between 4 and 5 percent of all active offenders, frequently and consistently commits crimes across several years, and sometimes for decades. As a result, its members are considered career offenders (DeLisi 2001). Their criminal careers, characterized by the "longitudinal sequence of crimes committed by an individual offender" (Blumstein 1986, 12), in many ways resemble legitimate careers; both involve onset, ongoing participation in their occupation-specific activities, a long-term duration, and eventual cessation (Tunnell 1992, 2; Gadd and Farrall 2004; Sampson and Laub 2003). Unlike most individuals who dabbled in street crimes in their youth, this group's criminal behaviors remain mostly unaffected by maturation. Rather, their predatory offending typically escalates in both frequency and seriousness across several, yet often interrupted, years of active crime commission. Even so, as research conclusively shows, even these offenders eventually desist (see, e.g., Farrington 2003; Sampson and Laub 2003).

One early study on the pervasiveness of criminal involvement found that 25 percent of a sample of 624 offenders had committed 60 percent of the armed robberies and burglaries (Peterson et al. 1980). Likewise, the sixty male property offenders of Tunnell's (1992, 28) study were frequently and repetitively active and committed a reported total of 48,726 crimes across their careers. Considering that fewer than sixty of the sample engaged in any one specific crime type (e.g., only twenty-nine committed armed robberies and only forty-three committed residential burglaries), the average number of specific offenses by type informs us more precisely of their criminal activity. For example, twenty-nine individuals committed 37 armed robberies on average; seventeen men averaged 53 strong armed robberies; forty-three participants committed 116 residential burglaries and 56 business burglaries on average; and an average of 101 shopliftings were committed by forty individuals. These figures indicate extreme activity in the most serious and costly predatory index crimes.

A recent study from Sweden indicates likewise, suggesting cross-national similarities. For example, data show that Swedish chronic offenders begin their criminal activities at an earlier age than others and are responsible for the largest proportion of more serious offenses such as robbery and theft (Svennson 2002).

In almost every case, and reported in research from a number of countries, adult criminals began committing illicit activities during their youth. Self-report data consistently show that young people of every social class, race, and religion commit deviant and criminal acts and that these offenses peak between ages fifteen and nineteen (see, e.g., Farrington 1986; Wolfgang, Thornberry, and Figlio 1987). Those young people who participate in the most serious offenses (e.g., robbery) are much likelier to continue committing crimes into their adulthood. Participation in particularly serious first offenses indicates a high risk of continued criminality and pathways into criminal careers.

Research shows too that chronic offenders are those who have had contact with the criminal justice system at an earlier age (for example, age sixteen) than one-time or occasional criminals. For example, if an individual's first conviction is for a serious offense (e.g., robbery), they have a 19 percent chance of becoming a chronic offender. If an individual's first and second convictions are for a serious offense, the chances of their habitually committing crime are elevated to 60 percent (Svennson 2002). The interactive effects of early onset, crime choice, and contact with the criminal justice system may be especially salient to the likelihood of sustained criminal activity.

Theoretical explanations for chronic criminality are addressed in chapter 6. But an important issue at this point is that learning criminal behaviors and definitions favorable to them within a social context supportive of both definitions and behaviors is central to the onset of routinely committing crime. Routine activities, such as unstructured interaction with peers in the absence of authority figures, provide opportunities for both learning and acting. This differential association and social context thesis is supported by research conducted in various countries and is discussed further in chapter 6 (see, e.g., Bernburg and Thorlindsson 2001). Of importance here is that these socially developed definitions contribute to participation in crime among young people, some who will continue to commit crimes well into adulthood and who are the subject of this book.

Although a host of research has been conducted on groups of repetitive property offenders, their careers, and ultimate cessation (see, e.g., Glueck and Glueck 1968; Wolfgang, Figlio, and Sellin 1972; Sampson and Laub 1993; Laub and Sampson 2003), little direct attention of late has been given to an issue central to these young criminals and their marginal existence—social class. Beyond this sociologically fundamental, yet sometimes overlooked, background variable, a focus on crime's foreground also is necessary. It includes financial rewards, lifestyles, and identities that are culturally or, more precisely, subculturally defined as compelling, attractive, pleasurable, sensual, and worthy of risky decisions and behaviors. This book's treatment of class, culture, and consciousness links the background of persistent offenders' social class to the foreground of criminal lifestyles, shared meanings, and crime-as-action.

Frequent participation in crime obviously is not solely limited to street criminals. By comparison, some white-collar offenders evidently break the law repetitively. Research on white-collar crime since Sutherland's (1949) landmark study consistently indicates that a core group of corporations repeatedly engages in illicit behavior (Hagan 1994, 107). Thus, the term *chronic offender* is applicable to both white-collar and street criminals.

Although white-collar professionals enjoy a privileged position and have a genuine stake in conformity, they nonetheless are willing to jeopardize the trust endowed to them by participating in illegal activities. But disagreement remains over whether they have more or less to lose from criminal sanctions than dispossessed property offenders. The latter group has less to lose than corporate offenders to begin with and, as a result, perhaps more to lose from punishment processes. Research into both white-collar and street crime suggests that social class is relevant to crime and delinquency and the social response "in interesting, albeit complicated, ways" (Hagan 1994, 110).

Indisputable evidence shows that street criminals are punished more severely for their crimes than white-collar offenders (see, e.g., Benson and Cullen 1998). In fact, nearly every resource in the criminal justice system is earmarked for controlling street crimes. Meanwhile, the financial costs associated with street crimes are dwarfed compared to those of white-collar offenders. In both cases though, social class remains a central element for understanding the crime's background and foreground, the type of crime selected, the offender's rationale and opportunity, and the response of the criminal justice system.

Lower-class members are disproportionately represented in arrest data for both serious violent and property crimes. Arrest data indicate that they also are overrepresented in cases of sexual assault and auto theft for financial gain. Joyriding among young people, however, is equally prevalent across social classes. On the other hand, individuals engaged in occupational, and especially organizational offenses, typically are higher-income persons of a different social class. Their crimes are committed within legitimate occupations and work settings and "require rank-specific opportunities for offending" (Miethe and McCorkle 1998, 234).

White-collar criminals are privileged and are responded to differently in part because criminal intent is difficult to infer to their illegalities. In the main, white-collar offenders deny that criminal intent is a part of their actions. They claim that harmful consequences from their behaviors are due to, for example, mistakes, oversights, and poor communication. This position is often rhetorical when suggested that executives never intend to kill or maim workers or consumers; they do not mean to kill or severely alter ecosystems; and they do not intentionally poison the air and ground water. These positions are refuted when treating intent as a reflection of behavior and, especially, repetitive behavior. If, as the reasoning goes, one intentionally and continually violates the law by placing workers in harm's way, by manufacturing faulty and dangerous products, or by secretly dumping toxic wastes, the consequences from such patterned and unlawful behavior suggest intent. The consequences should surprise no one (see, e.g., Coleman 1985).

When discovered, white-collar offenders often suggest that only one part of their life is under scrutiny—the crime (Benson 1985). This claim, to some degree, is status management aimed at preventing further degradation in rank. Property offenders likewise suggest the same and consider themselves more complex than the oft-applied and disparaging status of convicts. White-collar criminals, relying on various neutralization techniques, also define their actions as necessary within the realities of the contemporary business world. Beyond social-psychological benefits that they derive from such stated positions, there seemingly is an attempt to convince the victim, the authorities, and society that their actions are excusable behaviors of savvy businessmen (white-collar offenders, like serious property offenders, most often are male).

This justification is also dominant among property offenders. They, too, claim their actions are necessary, which aids in neutralizing their conceptualizations of self and behavior. Furthermore, like white-collar offenders, they imply, through their rationalizations, that they desire greater understanding than the simple one offered by criminal justice system workers, members of the mass media, and politicians.

A central thread running through both street and suite crime is the relevance of class to offenses committed to maintain class-based and culturally defined lifestyles. White-collar crimes often are performed for economic or status advantages or to prevent economic or status loss. In these cases, illegal behaviors evidently are defined as advantageous or necessary. Property crimes frequently are committed for immediate financial gain, sustenance, thrills, or drug addictions demanding regular attention. White-collar offenders enjoy an affluent, class-advantaged lifestyle, while property offenders live altogether differently—as disadvantaged, lower-class members. Individual white-collar offenders who, for example, engage in embezzlement define their situations as extraordinary and explain their actions as a response to their unusual circumstances. Property criminals who steal from their neighbors define their situations similarly. For example, embezzlers may rationalize their actions as resulting from their low salaries or because they deserve the money (Benson 1985). They also suggest that their offenses result from their extraordinary financial circumstances and personal debt. These unusual circumstances are class based; they suggest that "high levels of personal indebtedness are a common feature of male white-collar offenders compared with garden variety offenders and with citizens generally" (Levi 1994, 239). Indebtedness is rarely linked to repetitive property offenders. Rather, their unusual (and largely deviant) circumstances, their lack of legitimate opportunities, and their pressing daily need for cash explain their participation in crime far more than among white-collar offenders. White-collar workers enjoy advantages, such as supportive social networks, that exceed those of underclass property offenders.

In both cases—street and suite crimes—offenders display specific lifestyle concerns that are related to their crimes of choice and, more importantly, to their social class and cultures. Class plays as much a part in precipitating the unusual circumstances within which they find themselves as it does in their range of solutions. Class informs actors of the crime type that is possible to commit or even contemplate. Class thus determines their circumstances, both usual and unusual, and the range of possibilities, both legitimate and illegitimate, for addressing them. For as much as some poor people (or working-class people, for that matter) may want to engage in profitable acts such as embezzlement, they simply do not have the opportunity. Their class location prohibits participating in a potentially lucrative crime and determines the narrow range of criminal activities available to them. Street criminals' problem "is not that they do crimes while others do not. Their problem is that they do not do so from a position of power" (Chambliss 1987, 6). This is problematic for them in terms of financial pay-off and in the degree of the criminal justice system's response to them and their activities.

Across this book, issues central to lower-class, persistent, property offenders are described to highlight background factors, lifestyles, and constructions of reality at the foreground of crime. Class, culture, and consciousness are crucial variables for understanding frequent and repetitive participation in crime. As the above discussion shows, class is relevant to street and white-collar crime.

As is revealed in the next chapter, class, as a concept, has recently been criticized for offering little explanatory utility. This book takes another position by suggesting that class is relevant to crimes of theft, whether in the streets or in the suites. Nonetheless, this book's focus is on property theft among street criminals and their class location, class-based opportunities, lower-class criminal subcultures, and lower-class criminal lifestyles.

2

SOCIAL CLASS
AND PROPERTY CRIME

Contemporary sociology is witnessing a renewed assessment of social class and its relevance to everyday life. Some recent research, using various assumptions and methodologies, locates class within community and subcultural orientations; for others, class and everyday life are best explained within political-economic contexts (Hagedorn 1988; Wilson 1987; Hagan 1994). Although questions about the significance of class to a late- or postmodern sociology and, more specifically, to sociologies of crime have been raised, dismissing class and its relevance to social life is not supported by the evidence.

Recent questions, such as, "What's class got to do with it?" first must be preceded by more fundamental queries, such as, "What is class? How are classes, especially the poor and working classes, differentiated (differences that recently have converged in some contemporary social science)? And how are these distinctions relevant to property crime and criminals?" (Hagan and Peterson 1995). Although perhaps not as welcome as in the past, these questions remain central to a sociology of crime. In my estimation, they are especially germane to the most serious and lucrative property crimes—burglary and armed robbery—and to those most serious property offenders—persistent criminals.

Questions of this nature are especially pertinent given that contemporary academic writing on class and its relevance to street crime often seemingly confuses the working class with the poor, or in today's vernacular, the underclass (and yesterday's lumpen proletariat).[1] Various texts and research monographs, cutting across the political landscape, refer to working-class crime and criminals, even "intra-working class crime," without offering nominal or operational definitions of *working class* and leaving readers to assume the implied meanings (Lea and Young 1984; DeKeseredy, MacLean,

7

and Schwartz 1997). But, if these texts refer to what working class has meant throughout industrial and postindustrial world history, then a closer examination of the use of this concept and a determination of its connection to crime commission and victimization are needed.

The working class is materially and qualitatively different from the underclass (although within popular political-economic dialogues in the United States, such distinctions often are disregarded) (Gans 1995; E. Wright 1985; 1997). Likewise, the type and frequency of crimes committed by the working class are as different from underclass offenses as they are to corporate transgressions. Yet, crime in America is too often misdiagnosed as a working-class phenomenon.[2]

Consider, for a moment, working-class acquaintances and to what extent they currently are involved in crime or to what extent they were involved in their youth. Like most individuals, they were probably mixed up in minor infractions during their youth but presently are not involved in crime. Researchers know, and have known for decades largely from self-report data, that youth crime cuts across demographic categories of race, ethnicity, religious affiliation, and social class. As well established as this finding is, researchers also recognize that most young people, during their late teens, stop committing crime (Steffensmeier and Allan 1995). But a central focus of this book is on those who continue participating in crime into and across adulthood. What about their race, ethnicity, religious affiliation, and social class? And what do we know about the types of crimes they commit? Regarding the latter, we know that they gravitate toward the more serious garden-variety crimes (Rand 1987; Farrington 2003). With reference to the former, we know that race, gender, and social class are directly related. Evidence consistently shows that underclass males and minorities, more so than other social groupings, are disproportionately implicated in more serious property crimes.

Although working-class adults may dabble in crime, especially if their economic conditions worsen (e.g., they become and remain unemployed), they likely do not do so with the frequency of the chronically unemployed. There is little evidence supporting the notion that worsening economic conditions propel working-class adults into criminal misdeeds. Unemployed working-class adults generally have access to other sources of income and emotional support (e.g., financially secure extended families). In other words, they have class-based advantages that are not as readily available to underclass members and their families (Young 1997, 31).

Employment is a significant factor in predicting participation in crimes. Individuals who work generally do not commit property crimes.

Even those who have been involved in crimes, once employed, discontinue their illegal behaviors. Recent longitudinal research supports the employment-desistance thesis. Employment evidently is a key transition in the life course and is related to reductions in (and often desistance from) both crime and drug use. Research suggests that employment provides financial and social incentives for ceasing criminal and antisocial behavior. Social bonds and pro-social relations develop from employment and result in the elimination of previous deviant peer networks (Cullen and Wright 2004). Working is most often a factor in adjudicating class location. As is shown later in this chapter, the underclass (where, arguably, chronic offenders reside) is without work.

Some scholarship treats social class as impertinent and irrelevant. Other scholarship considers social class central to any appreciation of the social. Although its relevance has varied across currents of sociological thought, social class has been (and remains) a fundamentally important concept for the social sciences. It is complimented when linked to additional social facts such as gender, race, culture, biography, and ideology, none of which diminishes the relevance and the reality of social class. Social class remains central to our knowledge of criminalization, crime, criminals, criminal opportunity, and the objectives and operations of the criminal justice system. Across the past several decades of research on the sociology of crime, social class (under a variety of operational definitions) may have received as much treatment as any single variable.

Today, though, class is under attack and theoretical attention to it has dwindled (Hagan 1994). Given the attention to conflicts over race and gender, and as rhetoric about those issues has become fashionable, class may have become "the uncool subject" (hooks 2000, vii). Two recent book titles, however, make the claim that class is central to intellectual debates and lived realities. Eric Olin Wright's (1997) research monograph, *Class Counts*, and the recent publication by influential author bell hooks (2000), *Where We Stand: Class Matters*, are important works on the relevance of class to social life and biography.

ADJUDICATING CLASS

Social class has been nominally and operationally defined in a variety of ways. Some mainstream approaches use socioeconomic status, income, education, occupation, and parents' income. Beyond these definitions, *class*, for Marx, is adjudicated by relationships to the means of production; and for

Weber, it is arbitrated by participation in consumption, or by one's relationship to the market (Weber 1968, chap. 4; E. Wright 1985; 1997). The Marxian distinction of adjudicating class by relationship to the means of production is "to show that the way each class relates to the mode of production will determine the way those classes relate to one another politically and economically" (Lynch and Groves 1989, 11). Thus, those holding privileged class positions are isolated from economic concerns and political impotence that are often characteristic of those in less privileged positions. Interclass relations, from this conceptualization, are hierarchical.

Weber, using the market or consumption rather than production as the defining adjudication of class, emphasizes such variables as life chances, lifestyles, and political conflicts over power (i.e., Macht) rather than simply economic advantages based on property ownership or nonownership (Walliman et al. 1980). Weber, in his class-party-status triplet, arguably has pointed to "the most significant possible stratification orders" (Pakulski and Waters 1996, 24). Stratification, within a Weberian analysis, emphasizes status groups that share a common way of life. As a concept, status groups are as important as social class is to other interpretations. For Weber, then, class is best "analysed in terms of power, where class, status and party are the three principal forms of institutionalized power distribution" (Pakulski and Waters 1996, 29). Class relations within a Weberian analysis are not a simple unidimensional phenomenon but are always interconnected in complex ways with other features of social structure. "The social fabric always involves a warp of class relations and a weft of status relations and a rich embroidery of associative relations" (Pakulski and Waters 1996, 29–30).

Class, according to neo-Weberian and other contemporary interpretations, is undoubtedly a much more complex and dynamic concept than Marx iterated. And social divisions entail more than simple production relationships. But, extrapolating from these conceptualizations, we can assume that privileged members of society have unique relationships to production *and* consumption. They possess status and power unavailable to dispossessed members of society and to those dispossessed whose master status includes ex-con, drug addict, or welfare mother (among others).

The research of Eric Olin Wright focuses on the adjudication and empirical realities of social class in America (compared to Sweden). Operationally defining the working class in terms of exploitation, it undoubtedly is the central class exploited in the production process as surplus value is expropriated from its labors (E. Wright 1985, 195). Exploitation is central to social class adjudication for Wright (and Marx and Weber) and work is a precursor to expropriative exploitation. Social class in capitalist societies is based on "the complex intersection of three forms of exploitation: exploitation based on the ownership of capital assets, the control of organization assets and the possession of skill or credential assets" (E. Wright 1985, 283).

In other words, class determines who gets what and why.

This assessment, based on operationally powerful definitions and empiricism, draws from both Marx and Weber, includes power and status, and adjudicates class distinctions. It implies that the underclass is the displaced category, having no relationship to production processes or control of organizational or credential assets. The underclass remains materially and qualitatively different from the working class.

Relevant to these distinctions, class location is fundamental for determining individuals' objective possibilities and the concrete alternatives available to them when making decisions. On the one hand, "this concerns what Weber referred to as the individual's 'life chances,' the overall trajectory of possibilities individuals face over the life cycle." On the other hand, "it concerns the daily choices people face about what to do and how to do it" (E. Wright 1985, 144). This conceptualization refers to members of any and every social class. It refers to opportunity, alternatives (both real and perceived), and motive. Furthermore, it is applicable to groups and individuals who participate in either legitimate or illegitimate activities. It is squarely relevant to situational choices made by both individuals and organizations, and it is applicable to both property and white-collar crimes.

Class is relevant for understanding criminals and their choices that are determined, in part, by their class and their associative yet differentially distributed status and power-based opportunities.

ONGOING CLASS DEBATES

Reminiscent of Mark Twain's observation that news of his own death had been greatly exaggerated, a recent publication declared the death of social class (Pakulski and Waters 1996). Although an overstatement, this assessment has some grain of truth. Class *is* no longer as central to politics and scholarship as it once was. Other divisive social forces have challenged its place—"the right is turning its attention to morality and ethnicity while the critical left is becoming increasingly concerned about issues of gender, ecology, citizenship and human rights" (Pakulski and Waters 1996, 1). However important and apropos these social forces are to the social sciences, none adequately explains group divisions resulting from production and consumption exchanges and their associated economic and political power and status differentials.

Class analysis may have become less important because of social scientists' distance from those holding class positions beneath their own. This effectually limits exposure to and understanding of others' existence and cultures. Their biographies and daily encounters with structures and processes are foreign to outsiders' experiences.

In some cases, social class is simply ignored. In others, class and class analyses are criticized as limited in scope and as overly deterministic. This criticism is, to some extent, accurate. Furthermore, those once widely accepted determinates of class have proven increasingly nebulous as classes emerge and fade away, as lines of demarcation shift, and as social, economic, and political milieus take on their own historical features differing significantly from earlier class explications.

Once relevant, class today is passed off, by some, as passé. But there seems to be a willingness to merely give up on class as a central concept, and in sociology, giving up on a social explanation is nearly unprecedented. Class as a concept may not have worked all that well; it's been difficult to operationalize and measure, and it currently appears irrelevant to U.S. politics and no longer central to Eastern European cultures. But understanding the social has never been a simple procedure in part because of the politicized nature of sociological concepts and the process of doing sociology. The very objects of sociology itself, according to Bourdieu (1993, 9), "are stakes in social struggles," and class, as an explanatory concept, is unparalleled in tapping into the sociopolitical. Class is not just another stake in social struggle; it has been and remains one of the big stakes in ongoing social struggles. Rather than regarding class as dead, sociological knowledge likely will benefit if we continue struggling, especially in the face of mounting academic and political apathy, with its use as a descriptive and analytical concept. Recent and more holistic ventures emphasize multicollinearity, with class as a *central* explanatory variable (see, e.g., Vold, Bernard, and Snipes 2002, chap. 5).

Critics claim that class analyses limit sociological inquiry. The class perspective is treated as a political straightjacket that impedes a realistic appreciation of contemporary social life, politics, and culture. The supporting claim is that classes are dissolving "and that the most advanced societies are no longer class societies" (Pakulski and Waters 1996, 4). Although these criticisms acknowledge ongoing social inequalities and divisions, it is assumed that conflicts are based on divisive issues other than social class. The logic is that most contemporary struggles around the world have little to do with class and much more to do with race, ethnicity, gender, religion, the environment, and sexual preferences. As a result, most contemporary conflicts are "issue-oriented and territorially based." Sociology, it is argued, is doing itself an injustice by continuing to rely on a concept that "died somewhere between the beginning of the twentieth century and the end of the Great Depression" (Pakulski and Waters 1996, 20, 23, and 26).[3]

Although compelling, such arguments ignore a vast and growing body of recent literature. Qualitative and quantitative research clearly indicates that class remains a central divisive issue, one that is alive and well in both urban and rural areas. For example, the works of William Julius Wilson (1987; 1997), Mercer Sullivan (1989), and Joan Moore (1991), empirically substantiate the relevance of class, capital disinvestment, social isolation, cultural adaptation, chronic adult unemployment, and the growing underclass to current social problems, especially within metropolitan areas. Larger cities, especially in the Middle Atlantic and Midwest regions, "tend to have far more concentrated poverty problems (neighborhoods with poverty rates of 40 percent or more) than their suburban counterparts." Furthermore, "a much higher proportion of the poor in central cities are black or Hispanic" (Mangum, Mangum, and Sum 2003, 45). Class is central to each of those studies and to these recent data.

Class—its composition, size, and relevance in space and time—is affected by political and economic forces at work from within and without cities, communities, blocks, and boroughs. For example, deliberate and intentional discriminations in American housing policies (both historically and currently), race, and social class coalesce as explanation for the development of urban underclass neighborhoods (Massey and Denton 1993). Likewise, class is useful for explaining lifestyle, choice, and risk-taking behaviors among both street and corporate criminals.

Social science that is skeptical about (or perhaps hostile to) a class analysis may find it advantageous to simply dismiss class as a nonissue, an atavistic concept, a dead canon. Ironically, nearly every other social phenomenon is embraced as partial explanation for crime—social ecology, opportunity, race, gender, age, culture, biography, population density, you name it—with the lone exception of class. It has nearly become an untouchable and its dismissal has the potential, we are cautioned, to impoverish criminology (Hagan 1992, 1). Class may no longer be *the* proto-social explanation, but it, along with gender and age, comprises a powerful trinity of sociological discourse without which we would know precious little about adult crime, criminals, and victimization.

THE CLASS-CRIME CONNECTION

Conducted over decades, research conclusively shows that class, gender, and age represent the three most important variables associated with crime, criminalization, crime trends, and victimization. While street crime is linked to age and gender, the most salient feature "is its link to the concentration of poverty," particularly within inner cities—a class-crime connection (Hagan and Peterson 1995, 20). Research consistently shows that the street criminals in the United States of most concern—persistent offenders—share one commonality: they are poor (Currie 1996, 37–38).

Poverty's connection to crime is complex. Poverty and crime also are empirically linked in other countries that, like the United States, are characterized as a "market society" (rather than simply a "market economy"), within which material, cultural, symbolic, and psychic needs are organized by and subordinated to private gain (Currie 1997, 37). Poverty, in the midst of plenty, is the leading correlative variable with adult property crimes; gender (or, more precisely, "public masculinity") is running in a very close second place (Messerschmidt 1993, chaps. 4 and 5).

Persistent criminals share a similar culture, status, lifestyle, and worldview that shape their common perceptions and decisions about crime and its relevance to subsistence, thrills, and high living. These commonalities result, in part, from their class location; repetitive criminals are a part of today's under- rather than working class.

Most of our knowledge about chronic offenders comes from those who have come under the control of the criminal justice system. For example, research shows that 70 to 75 percent of all state prisoners are illiterate and only one-third completed high school. Literacy proficiency, identified as a Level 3 benchmark, is considered a minimum for success in contemporary labor markets. Recent surveys of state prisoners report that 70 percent perform at below a Literacy Level 3 ("Correctional education facts" 2004). Reportedly, more than half had earned less than $10,000 prior to their arrest and subsequent incarceration (about $9,000 annually is the poverty threshold for a one-member household) (DiMascio 1995; Mangum et al. 2003). Also, among state prisoners, 43 percent had earned less than a GED, while a paltry 2.7 percent were college graduates ("Correctional education facts" 2004).

The recently raised question by some in criminology—"What's class got to do with it?"—expresses "a skepticism about the connection of class with crime that distinguishes them from other scholars as well as laypersons" (Hagan 1992, 1). In other words, this question places their assumptions about class and crime out of step with widespread beliefs that pervade both academic and nonacademic worldviews. Those who consider class peripheral, or who may have abandoned the class–crime assumption, point to a weak to nonexistent statistical correlation from self-report data with individual adolescents (Hagan 1992, 3). These findings are nothing new. Historically, the class–crime connection among *young people* has been dubious since criminal participation among the young is not class specific. Among young people, gender (or public masculinity) rather than class is perhaps the most important link with delinquency. Among adults, sustained and repetitive criminal behavior likely has more to do with social class.

Research on etiology and focusing on a class–crime relationship has used self-report data from samples of young people. The methodology itself may have contributed to the studies' own shortcomings. These research findings contradict long-held assumptions about class–crime connections and differ from evidence generated from a host of ethnographic and community-based studies with adults (Hagan 1996). Social class has much stronger relationships to persistence and frequency of crime commission into adulthood than to etiology among the young. Other factors, such as age, gender, peer pressure, differential association, and a lack of internal and external control, likely explain etiology among the young. As these other factors' effects on criminal participation are neutralized with age, responsibilities, control, and increased opportunities, class emerges as the most relevant to those who continue participating in predatory crimes into their adult years and with increased frequency and severity.

As pervasive as youth crime is in American culture, the focus of this book (and that of other recent studies on property crime in the United States) is on adults who repetitively commit crime with increased frequency and seriousness. Those who continue committing crime beyond adolescence are usually poor males. Thus, as is shown throughout this work using primary and secondary data, both class and gender are crucial variables for understanding the actions, careers, cultures, and consciousness of persistent property offenders. Although crime is linked to age (among other variables), we cannot ignore "a set of social conditions, of which persistent poverty is a part," and which propels individuals and sustains their activity into a life of repetitively committing serious property crimes (Currie 1996, 37). These conditions and poverty are directly relevant to the social class issue.

Elliott Currie (1996, 38) describes the synergistic effects of poverty on "other social institutions—especially on the stability and cohesiveness of family and community" as compelling explanations for serious and repetitive crime in the United States primarily, and secondarily in other advanced countries characterized as market societies. These effects, coupled with structured political and economic changes (both nationally and globally), are connected to growing numbers of underclass members, criminogenic places, and the entrenchment of vice service centers, criminal opportunities, socially disorganized communities, and motivated offenders with little stake in conformity or commitment to legitimacy.

THE UNDERCLASS AND CRIME

No matter how class may be operationally defined or the number of classes adjudicated, it seems doubtful that any scheme could ignore the existence of an economically and culturally marginalized group—the underclass—within which are located (among other groups) clusters of repetitive and persistent adult property offenders. Today's underclass is composed of surplus populations of the useless proletariat (Marx and Engels 1948, 20). Its relationship to production and consumption is unique: it has no (or nearly no) involvement with the means of production and only participates peripherally in market consumption, although perhaps to a larger extent within underground economies (Williams and Kornblum 1985).

Although without a place in legitimate production-consumption processes, the underclass theoretically remains necessary for the continued expansion of capital accumulation (and in recent years, increasingly within both public and private crime control industries). It is composed of the expendables of society. It is a population cast off by systemic forces and it survives by means other than working for a wage. Its existence is a structural phenomenon, the result of streamlining production processes that excludes groups of individuals from participating in the production (and, to a large extent, the consumption) of goods and services yet who are exposed daily to a consumer culture.

Poverty and relative deprivation are central to understanding the poor's cultures, ways of life, and their unique subcultural consciousness that differs from that of other classes. Poverty and relative deprivation (which also receives attention in chapters 4 and 6) are economic forces that contribute to generating populations of criminally active individuals whose criminal participation increases in frequency and seriousness into adulthood (Young 1992a).[4]

Karl Marx (1981) viewed crime, in relation to the development of capitalism, as a law violation by those who had little choice but crime for their livelihood. Crime, then, often is committed by those displaced by the growth of capitalism.[5] Writing of *free will* (e.g., freely choosing to commit a crime), Marx (1981) critically suggests that this concept ignores material conditions and the differences in one group's conditions over another. To understand people's participation in crime, we should examine the concrete social circumstances in which they are situated. This implies that some individuals, to survive or, more precisely, to consume, have few choices other than illegal ones. Some may be as "free" not to choose crime as a means of existence as the working class is free not to choose wage labor as a means of subsistence.

Although John Hagan (1992, 1) suggests that old labels, such as "dangerous" and "criminal classes," as well as new ones, such as "underclass," are pejorative and may be problematic, he makes a bold argument for keeping class central to our analyses of crime; to do otherwise denies one of the most important traditions and analytical concepts of the social sciences. And although race in the United States is central to any discussion of class, crime, victims, and the subjects of the criminal justice system, it is often approached cautiously. The apprehension is that public misinterpretations may result in a conceptual transformation of the nonwhite underclass "from surplus and discarded labor into an exclusive group of black urban terrorists" (Marks 1991, 454). Gans (1995, 13) also advises clarity with rhetoric and social research by observing that: "This being America, with its taboo against class terminology, popular private communication uses racial and ethnic labels far more often than class ones."

Likewise, focusing solely on norm violations of the poor, rather than on structural antecedents for their economic conditions and life choices, may result in conceptually transforming the underclass into an undeserving mass of faceless individuals who may be defined as lacking the ability to conform (Gans 1995). For example, a class-based manifestation of the urban underclass is its affiliation with crime (Hagan 1992). Although most underclass individuals do not commit crime, it nonetheless is often seen as a distinct characteristic of underclass occupants. Other traits of underclass individuals (and, unfortunately, often the only ones observable by the nonpoor) include participating in underground economic enterprises, receiving welfare assistance, engaging in drug abuse, or simply retreating—each, in the way it manifests itself, is a class-based adaptation to inequalities.

Relevant to these manifestations of social class is status. For the most part, the underclass experiences a negative standing imposed on them by others. The underclass, "composed of welfare dependents, marginalized service workers, post colonial migrants . . . and workers disadvantaged by age, ethnicity or gender" is a class that includes the "racially stigmatized, the unemployable, and permanent state dependents" (Pakulski and Waters 1996,

58). In other words, these groupings are defined not only by class but also by status, and a publicly degraded one at that.

YOUTH, RACE, AND STATUS

The importance of class to crime is revealed in the linkages between crime and inequality that "occupy a central place in the social organization of American society, as well as other nations" (Hagan and Peterson 1995, 14). Furthermore, crime and its impact on individuals not only adversely effects individual relations but often polarizes class relations (Hagan and Peterson 1995, 15). Although conceptualizations of class and crime may require further refinement and sophistication, the facts nonetheless "confirm that delinquency, crime and contacts with the criminal justice system are massive risk factors in the lives of poorly educated and economically disadvantaged black youth and young adults"—a class-race-crime connection (Hagan and Peterson 1995, 17).

This connection is well documented in the realities of the everyday operations of the criminal justice system. Police report defining youth of color as threatening and hostile. Individuals' demeanor and behavior influence police decision-making. Evidence shows that antagonistic suspects are more likely to be arrested than deferential ones. Officers typically require receiving "more deference than they give" (Hagan and Peterson 1995, 25). For example, police desire being referred to as "officer" but may refer to citizens by their first names or "son" or "boy."

Beyond differential surveillance and treatment given to individuals, particular places or areas of town are policed much heavier than others. This is especially the case within depressed, inner-city areas where residents are largely poor minorities. Due to crowded conditions and dense urban living, taken-for-granted private activities become public and are much more likely to be observed by others, including the police. Densely populated, underclass areas impose upon residents a particular type of community organization that is "characterized by a high level of mutual surveillance." This organization affects residents' privacy by making their activities, whether licit or illicit, public. "The same act detected, reported, and recorded as illegal in a densely populated minority community may go undetected, unreported, and unrecorded in less densely populated middle- and upper-class settings" (Hagan and Peterson 1995, 27).

Once areas are defined as "offensible space" or "hot spots," police have reason enough for increasing surveillance and arresting suspicious individuals for activities that in an earlier time (and in a different space) would have gone unnoticed. Furthermore, with the number of people being sent to prison increasing nearly exponentially (from 500,000 in 1980 to 2,078,570 at midyear 2003), those netted in the war on crime are mostly the young, poor, and the nonwhite (Harrison and Karberg 2004).

Recent national data show that African American men are sentenced to prison at greater rates than any other racial category in the United States; African Americans comprise 44 percent of state and federal prisoners yet only 12 percent of the country's population. Likewise, Hispanics who represent only 10 percent of the U.S. population comprise 18 percent of prisoner population. Whites comprise 74 percent of the population and make up 36 percent of prisoners in the United States (DiMascio 1995, 13). At midyear 2003, there were 4,834 black males in prison or jails per 100,000 black males in the United States compared to 1,778 Hispanic male inmates per 100,000 Hispanic males and 681 white male inmates per 100,000 white males (Harrison and Karberg 2004). Given the race-class inequities in American society, "these facts are inconvenient for those who suggest that social class is unrelated to crime" (Chilton and Galvin 1985, 4).

When arrested and ensnarled in the machinations of the criminal justice system, the outcome can be devastating, especially for young people from disadvantaged backgrounds. Once an individual becomes involved in crime and encounters crime control agents, continued criminality as well as difficulties in finding legitimate work and exiting a life of crime may follow (Hagan 1994, 94).

Among sixty repetitive property offenders interviewed during one study (Tunnell 1992), the average age at first arrest was eleven. An arrest at a young age can set into motion offenders' frequent and continued contact with crime control industry officials and ongoing difficulties in conforming to legitimate societal expectations. As one underprivileged black male once said about his experiences with legal authorities, "There's one thing they don't mind doing here in this U.S. of A., is locking you up" (Private interview 1987).

Youth crime within industrialized countries is invariant. It is well documented that the young, having few legitimate opportunities for accessing money, yet inundated with images of consumable goods, are limited in options for participating in a consumption-driven society. Jobs available to them "make little use of their distinct advantages in muscular strength, physical endurance and sensual acuity" (Felson 1994, 80–81). Employment requisites and work expectations are vastly different for today's youth than for children of a century ago. Delinquency, especially among those apprehended, can affect one's life chances in various ways. Even an arrest without conviction can affect one's consciousness, opportunities, and lifestyle. For example, there is evidence that contacts with the criminal justice system have "especially negative effects for underclass males. Even if most underclass males who are arrested do not go to jail, the experience of arrest can have long-term, even intergenerational repercussions" (Hagan 1992, 10). These experiences have grave effects on life course trajectories. The greater and more frequent the contact with the criminal justice system, the more a young person has to overcome. When one is officially labeled a criminal offender, and recognized by the authorities as such, securing decent employment in poor communities with decreasing numbers of available blue-collar jobs becomes progressively more difficult. Research indicates that an arrest record can adversely affect one's employment chances and conditions as much as eight years later (Hagan 1994, 95). This was an often-heard theme among chronic property offenders of an earlier study (Tunnell 1992, 57). One burglar, for example, speaking about his experiences after his first prison incarceration, illustrates this well: "When you commit the crime, you commit it and you get sentenced to pay a debt to society. But that debt's never paid. You cannot pay that debt. You're screwed the rest of your life." His words, as others across recent studies, speak to the realities of age, class, race, crime, status, and exclusion.

RECENT RESEARCH ON THE
CLASS CRIME CONNECTION

Operational definitions of class invariably include economic indicators (e.g., income and wealth). Some definitions include employment status. The assumption is that an unemployed status indicates a social class qualitatively different from an employed one. As a result, research has investigated relationships between unemployment and street crime; some recent research findings support a relationship. Property crimes, such as burglary and robbery, and violent crimes, such as assault and homicide, are related to unemployment during historical periods of structural rather than frictional unemployment. In other words, research indicates a pronounced long-swing or cyclical pattern between unemployment and crime at the aggregate (Carlson and Michalowski 1997). This is an important finding about crime and an economic indicator that is assumed to measure worsening economic situations.

To date, however, little research on unemployment (as an indicator of social class) and crime exists using individuals as the unit of analysis and highlighting their lived experiences. Rather, the majority of research has used aggregate data focusing most often on the relationship between unemployment and youth. That body of research has been characterized as revealing "the expected correlation" between young peoples' unemployment and their participation in crime and delinquency, "even if the full nature of this correlation is only beginning to be understood" (Hagan 1992, 6).

Studies using aggregate data are problematic due to their ambiguous and, at times, contradictory findings. A recent review of over sixty studies, however, reports a consistent, "positive frequently significant relationship between unemployment and property crime [which] is strongest and most consistent when it is studied with time series data at the neighborhood level" (Hagan 1994, 88). From this evaluation of the existing body of research, the use of smaller units of analysis is supported more than aggregate data or the use of nations, for example, as units of analysis. But most research on the unemployment and crime question has not explored these issues with neighborhoods or individuals.

Research focusing solely on unemployment as an economic indicator and its relationship to crime in the United States typically has used aggregate data generated by the federal government. These numbers are incomplete accounts of national unemployment. They exclude, for example, the growing numbers of underemployed individuals who make up the working poor. Also excluded from official counts are college students and individuals younger than age eighteen or older than age sixty-five. Most alarming for understanding the relationship between crime and economic indicators is national data that excludes those who no longer report regularly to the Employment Security Administration. Excluded in the count, then, is the growing number of the chronically unemployed and those who have resigned themselves to living without work (except perhaps undocumented work or that within underground economies such as in deviance service centers).

Another important matter is that unemployment, for the majority of individuals officially counted as unemployed, is most often temporary. Those transiently unemployed likely have little impact on crime. After all, those officially counted as unemployed are more than likely working-class members who find themselves only intermittently unemployed. Unlike underclass members, they usually have the means for getting by during economic crises (e.g., a nest egg, other household members working, extended family members who can temporarily help). Furthermore, because of working-class individuals' commitment to conformity, they are unlikely to turn to crime when their economic situation temporarily worsens. They are much more likely to dutifully report to the Employment Security Office, file for unemployment benefits, and look for work.

The underclass and its members are not counted among the ranks of the officially unemployed. They are not drawing unemployment insurance checks; they are not reporting to the unemployment office on a regular basis for employment information. They are the chronically unemployed who have given up on finding decent-paying legitimate work and who remain excluded from official tallies. Thus, research examining the changing unemployment and crime issue that relies solely on official data is likely examining the wrong population. Those officially counted as unemployed likely have little effect on crime.

Sociology has only begun to describe just what unemployment means for those who are not a part of the officially documented unemployed. As a result, our knowledge is scant. But following the sociological tradition of using groups as the unit of analysis, some recent ethnographies of class and crime detail structural socioeconomic changes that some urban, minority, poor neighborhoods have experienced in recent years (e.g., the transition from industrial to service sector employment, the transition from full- to part-time employment, the exportation of jobs and capital flight, increasing unemployment and underemployment, and increasing isolation from cities' employment centers).

Mercer Sullivan's (1989) work, for example, shows that these changes are not what first motivate youth to engage in crime (since crime is committed by young people regardless of social class). Rather, those worsening economic conditions contribute to weak families and community controls which allow for differential association with deviant peers and routine deviant activities (Bernburg and Thorlindsson 2001). As a result, those youth who continue to routinely involve themselves in crime usually have greater difficulties in locating employment than those who mature out of it. This is especially the case given global economic and production changes and the harsh realities of disappearing work (Wilson 1997). Thus, while individual activities and structural changes explain ongoing criminal participation, political-economic policies manifest in worsening economic realities may play a part in setting into motion careers in crime.

Within communities, unemployment contributes to the onset of juvenile delinquency and it persists for those who continue committing crimes into adulthood. At the individual level (rather than the community level), delinquency contributes to adult unemployment which affects adult criminality (and chronic unemployment). "In other words, the diminished class circumstances of communities often establish conditions in which juvenile delinquency is linked to adult problems of unemployment and crime" (Hagan 1996, 12). Furthermore, subcultural delinquency among the young often results in educational difficulties and dropping out of school. Employment difficulties continue into adulthood and are manifest as despair and hopelessness (Hagan 1997).

Like Mercer Sullivan and John Hagan, William Julius Wilson (1987; 1997) describes political and economic policies that have had major impacts on the poorest enclaves within major American cities. His work describes capital flight, the loss of blue-collar jobs and others directly connected to blue-collar industry, the exodus of whites and middle-class blacks from urban centers, decreases in federal monies earmarked for cities and especially inner-city neighborhoods, decreases in locally generated tax revenues, and declining public spending on programs supporting urban neighborhoods' infrastructures. Meanwhile, federal dollars increasingly have been diverted toward affluent classes (nationally and internationally through, for example, the International Monetary Fund, tax breaks, public donations, corporate subsidies, and bail-outs). All told, these changes have created dramatic shifts in financial and capital holdings.

Poor neighborhoods have been left with dramatic increases in the number of unemployed youth within areas occupied almost solely by poor, unemployed adults. These neighborhoods' economies are closely tied to vice service centers. The neighborhoods hardest hit by these new structural formations and economic shifts are occupied mostly by people of color. Thus, poverty and race coalesce in inner-city neighborhoods, creating pools of desperate young men and women with little stake in conformity and who confront daily the harsh realities of urban angst, economic isolation, garden-variety criminal opportunities, and little else.

Related to these global changes effecting specific neighborhoods, Richard Wright and Scott Decker's (1994, 35; 1997) interview research with active, adult, residential burglars and armed robbers in East St. Louis shows important linkages between class and crime. In fact, all of their offenders were disproportionately poor, young, urban males. They were motivated to offend based on their perception of their current situations and alternatives. The foreground of their crimes was dominated by the necessity of meeting an immediate financial need. The decision to commit a specific burglary, for their subjects, developed when the offenders believed there was "a pressing need for cash" (Wright and Decker 1994, 36; 1997, 33). As other interview research supports, criminal decisions are shaped by both the daily realities of poverty and offenders' perceptions of limited opportunities. In other words, structure, agency, perceptions, and their ongoing social constructions of reality are crucial for understanding the activities of persistent burglars. Regarding such, Wright and Decker (1994, 48) make the following observation:

> Given the street corner context in which most burglary decisions were made, legitimate work did not represent a viable solution. . . . [They] . . . wanted money there and then and, in such circumstances, even day labor was irrelevant because it did not respond to the immediacy of their desire for cash. Moreover, the jobs available to most of the offenders were poorly paid and could not sustain their desired lifestyles.

They further report that the majority of their offenders desired lawful employment. In fact, 55 percent of the unemployed participants in their study who committed burglaries mostly for the money claimed they would stop offending "if someone gave them a good job" (Wright and Decker 1994, 49; 1997, 48). Their hope, especially given the realities of poverty and limited opportunity, is reminiscent of Paul Newman's portrayal of Butch Cassidy who, in that role, said, "If they'd pay me what they're spending to get me to stop robbing, I'd stop robbing." Like Cassidy, modern-day outlaws find few legitimate alternatives available that provide not only money but quick money as well as subculturally valued expressive rewards. Interview research with active armed robbers likewise shows high levels of unemployment—87 percent—indicating few legitimate financial courses of action exist for them as well (Wright and Decker 1997, 47).

Legitimate alternatives typically available to working- and middle-class people include borrowing money. But for underclass individuals (and especially those repetitively engaged in crime), borrowing is only a temporary solution to ongoing financial difficulties. For most people, it eventually becomes impossible as they bilk their few relatives and friends of cash. Borrowing, in their case, is a misnomer. The act is actually panhandling one's acquaintances who may find it difficult to refuse. In other words, it is no solution to their persistent needs. Consider the following conversations with two high rate burglars:

> Q. Did you think of anything else that you could do to get money, like borrow it?
> A. No. I'd done run that in the ground. See, you burn that up. That's burned up, right there, borrowing (Tunnell 1992, 65).

> Q. Did you consider doing anything else for money, at that time?
> A. I went to the bank four different times. I went to four or five different loan companies, you know the ones that say, "Come on in and

borrow money on your word" and all this. That's a crock of shit. They ain't anybody going to lend you nothing. I mean it's there for the taking, but it ain't there for the loaning (Tunnell 1992, 64–65).

Qualitative research (Tunnell 1992; Akerstrom 1985; Wright and Decker 1994) shows that persistent offenders generally participate in one or two types of crimes rather than engaging in a whole host of illegal activities. For example, burglary or armed robbery is often reported as criminals' "main line" (Wright and Decker 1997, 54). In other words, offenders report a commitment at least temporarily to a crime of specialty. In each case, given their ongoing needs for money and limited access to it, they mostly remain loyal to their primary criminal specialty; that is, the act that they know best and have learned is the most promising for generating income.

Regardless of which actions they may consider, persistent offenders as a group are restricted to class-bound and structurally limited opportunities. In other words, only limited types of illicit behavior are available (rather than those requiring legitimate power or prestige). Even if repetitive property offenders were employed, it is highly unlikely that they would hold positions that would allow them to engage in crimes of financial trust (e.g., embezzlement). Persistent offenders as a group lack skills necessary to bypass sophisticated security systems. They are not especially verbose and hence are unlikely to engage in lucrative crimes of fraud or con artistry. They mostly remain committed to their garden-variety property crimes requiring little skill and generating little payoff (Wright and Decker 1994, 54).

Linking class and criminal behavior to individuals' decisions and actions requires a consideration of their alternatives, perceived alternatives (which may be different from empirical choices available), and their assessment of the risks and rewards resulting from the contemplated variety of options.

The objective alternatives faced by individuals, however, are not directly transformed into actual choices or practices. Those objective alternatives must be perceived, the consequences (both material and normative) of different choices assessed, and a specific alternative chosen in light of such assessments. This process is partially the result of conscious, active, mental evaluations and calculations; it is partially the result of what Giddens refers to as 'practical consciousness,' the routinized ways people negotiate and understand their social world; and it is partially structured by largely unconscious psychological determinants. In any case, this subjectivity *mediates* the ways in which the objective conditions of class locations are translated into the active choices of class actions (E. Wright 1985, 145).

In other words, class location is a lens through which life chances and choices are filtered. Furthermore, this lens is perceptual—choices are made from one's empirical class location and these choices shape an individual's understanding and available possibilities. However, it is naïve to conceptualize offenders as reluctant participants driven to engage in crime due to their impoverished conditions and their need for the proverbial loaf of bread. Offenders, just as law-abiding poor people, obviously do not choose the economic conditions within which they exist. Yet, interestingly, they claim to spend most of their easily made fast cash on consumable items, such as alcohol and drugs, and secondarily on necessities, displaying a hedonistic "easy come easy go" lifestyle (Wright and Decker 1997, 43).

Since individuals engage in crime from various positions, opportunity is a crucial component for understanding any illegal behavior. For street criminals, class and a lack of social capital explain their involvement in their low-level crimes of choice. For white-collar criminals, an excess of social capital, primarily in the form of trust and respect, may explain their particular styles of illegalities (Hagan 1994, 101). Furthermore, "access to corporate resources is a unique advantage of class positions involving ownership and authority in business organizations. . . . [T]he social organization of work in the world of the modern corporation can itself be criminogenic" (Hagan 1994, 124). This arguably is the case given that dominant capitalist societies are "cultures of competition" affecting both white-collar offenses and street crimes (Coleman 1985).

Just as privileged positions and cultures of competition are criminogenic and provide an opportunity to engage in lucrative white-collar crimes, inaccessibility to paid work and social capital is also criminogenic. Class location determines access to participation in both street and suite crimes. As research shows, one needs "capital and organizational position to become a big-time white collar criminal" (Hagan 1994, 111). And unlike white-collar offenders, whose crimes are committed from positions of power, street crimes are committed from positions of powerlessness largely by the dispossessed. Class is central for explaining both crime types. Street and suite crimes "are different kinds of crime that likely have different connections to the concept of class" (Hagan 1994, 107).

Class is also relevant to both culture and consciousness. Furthermore, class is particularly useful for highlighting victimization, and it is relevant to discussions of various public policies and theoretical implications. These issues are covered in the following chapters.

NOTES

1. Although the term *underclass* is often used derisively, it is used here to describe growing numbers of individuals whose lives are shaped by the structural effects of market societies, their social exclusion, and the concentration effects of living in segregated, isolated communities (Wilson 1987; Peterson and Harrell 1992; Hagan 1994). Although underclass, as a label, is widely used at this time, it's use will likely fade away as emerging labels for the poor become legitimized by experts of one sort or another, and as the general public adopts such terminology (Gans 1995, 20–21).

2. Victims of crime undoubtedly are often working-class members. But this, in and of itself, does not necessarily mean that crime is a working-class phenomenon for such conceptualizations that disregard the other part of the crime equation—the criminal. Offenders central to this book and those considered the most serious—persistent criminals—are mostly located in the under—rather than working—class, as I argue throughout this chapter and book.

3. Replacing class with other issues is contrary to recent observations made by middle-class and affluent African Americans who emphasize how little they understand or have in common with poor, urban, criminally active young black males. Henry Louis Gates, for example, recently remarked that such urban criminals "might as well be from Mars" given the dissimilarities between his and their daily existences, cultures, and class.

4. C. Wright Mills (1956) and Michael Useem (1984) describe a subcultural consciousness inextricably wedded to lifestyles among elites. Mainstream sociology has long described "high-brow" and "low-brow" cultures resulting from and reflecting class and material conditions. Jack Katz (1988) described the sensual pleasures from wrongdoing central to criminal subcultures. More recently, Wright and Decker (1994) characterize criminals' lifestyle as a "party," meaning that their culture is dominated by thrills, drug use, excitement, and other sensual attractions of wrongdoing.

5. *Crime* is used here to refer to street or predatory crime rather than corporate or organizational crime. Organizational crime is elsewhere explained as a by-product of capitalist expansion or accumulation and committed on behalf of the organization by individuals in positions of power. Doubtless, individuals who commit street crimes do not commit crimes from positions of power. Their crimes often are explained in relation to their powerlessness or their exclusion from participating in capitalist enterprises and the labor force.

3

CULTURE AND PROPERTY CRIME

Regardless of the group, sociology recognizes that each has its own unique cultural attributes, some that are compatible with dominant culture, others that are deviant, and still others that are oppositional. Divergent groups differentiate themselves from one another by adopting distinct norms and by engaging in group-specific activities. The behaviors reinforce the culture or subculture. Sociology largely agrees that groups as diverse as priests and pimps, professional athletes and musicians, corporate executives and property offenders, although operating within dominant culture, have their own group attributes, values, styles, and normative systems (see, e.g., Ferrell 1995). In other words, they have developed their own group identity that sets them apart from both dominant culture and other subcultures.

Social class elucidates a great deal about adult males' career choices and their continued and frequent participation in property crimes. Long recognized and verified through interview research with active and once-active property offenders, culture, or, more precisely, subculture, accounts for much of their activity, decision-making, and commitment to street life and criminal careers. More specifically, to better appreciate the nuances of repetitive property offenders, an understanding of the cultures that they construct, through their interactions with both criminals and law-abiding citizens, and within which they function is necessary. It also is important to pay attention to their intermittent experiences with legitimate work and their reflections on and definitions of working for a wage, their constructions of public masculinities and attitudes and behaviors toward women, their commitment to free-spirited autonomy, their entrenchment in drug culture and their physiological and psychological addictions to various narcotics, and the sensual attractions of and rewards from engaging in serious property crimes.

This chapter describes these cultural attributes that dominate persistent property offenders' lives and to which they, to various degrees, are committed. Property offenders' subculture is described by highlighting the values, norms, philosophies, and worldviews that dominate their lives and that they have made public through interviews with researchers. This chapter focuses specifically on the following items that comprise a major part of property offenders' subcultures: their dislike for and inability to locate decent, legitimate work coupled with the immediacy of their needs and desires (and with little recognized distinction between the two); the importance they assign to street culture, fashion, and cool; the sensual pleasures they find at the foreground of committing crime; their persistent drug problems; their commitment to autonomy; and their sexism and constructions of public masculinities. Some of these traits are inseparable from their class location (such as their marginalization from the labor market), while others reflect something distinct—the cultural niche that they have carved out for themselves as representatives of bad-assed, free-spirited (and free-wheeling), drug-induced, street-centered anarchists, although with little ideological consciousness or political sophistication (this final point is developed further in chapter 4).

ATTITUDES ON AND REALITIES OF WORK

Adult repetitive property offenders are committed socially and economically to crime as a way of life. That life is characterized by long hours of boredom and monotony interrupted by brief periods of excitement, such as criminal, sexual, and deviant behavior (among others). Criminal behavior is expressively rewarding to individuals and groups committed to crime as a way of life. Yet, as research indicates, instrumental rewards are far more important (Tunnell 1992). Financial benefits, however, are not readily accessible.

Property criminals who are only marginally employable and who express unfavorable attitudes about work and its availability have few legitimate sources available. Property offenders, and especially those who have had contact with the criminal justice system, have little legitimate status. As a result, decent and well-paid legitimate work is not easily available to criminally active individuals who are committed to criminal subcultures.

When examining these empirical realities about property offenders, what is often overlooked are their attitudes about work, their perceptions on its availability, and the quality of life that it affords. Although some offenders appear to speak honestly about desiring well-paying jobs, others describe their disdain for legitimate employment, their refusal to participate in it, and their mocking condemnation of lawful citizens who work.

John Irwin (1980), among others, has observed that criminals consider their lifestyle more rewarding than a noncriminal way of life. This is especially the case when offenders face the realities of limited alternative life choices that are determined, in part, by their class location and their experiences with the criminal justice system. The following comment from a thirty-eight-year-old burglar is illustrative: "Jobs were hard to find, especially for a young man that didn't have no education and been in trouble" (Tunnell 1992, 56). Legitimate and well-paid opportunities are few in number for poorly educated, school dropouts with ex-con status who place much value in criminal activities and who are entrenched in criminal subcultures. Another interviewee's words are likewise insightful:

> I tried to find a job. But when you commit the crime, you commit it and you get sentenced to pay a debt to society. But that debt's never paid. You cannot pay that debt. You're screwed the rest of your life (Tunnell 1992, 57).

Two observations about the above statements are relevant. First, they reflect class location and the disadvantages associated with a lower-class position. In other words, structural restrictions offer some explanation for property offenders' exclusion from legitimate employment. Second, they reflect the realities of an ex-con master status and the resulting strictures on property offenders' abilities to excel in legitimate circles, including those of employment.

Beyond these two means by which entrenched property offenders are excluded from work are the attitudes and ideologies that they hold about employment, their definitions of it, and their assumptions about what it has to offer. For example, when contemplating whether to commit a crime, only seven among sixty property offenders considered legitimate behavior as an alternative. Also, forty-seven considered only another crime as an alternative behavior. An additional six stated that not only were they committed to doing nothing but crime, but they also would not consider legitimate work of any sort. In other words, they, in more adamant language than the others, rejected work and had little regard for it (Tunnell 1992). Consider the following dialogue:

> Q. You didn't used to work, did you?
> A. Not at all. I wouldn't work if you asked me to work. I thought it was other ways to do things besides working. I thought you were a fool

to work. "Why should you work, you fool? You ain't never going to have nothing." That's what I used to say.

Q. How about picking up an odd job for half a day?

A. Noooo. I thought I was too cool, too cool man. I thought I was too good. That would have been against my dignity to try to work. I wouldn't want nobody to know that I was doing that (Tunnell 1992, 61).

These words reflect a constant theme among property offenders across several published accounts and are indicative of a particular cultural attribute. For example, recent interview research with both active burglars and armed robbers shows that some offenders remain strongly opposed to legitimate work. A stated reason is that it adversely affects their way of life, which is street-centered and filled with leisure. Crime has such strong appeal to many because it allows them to "flaunt their independence from the routine imposed by the world of work" (Wright and Decker 1994, 48–49; see also Wright and Decker 1997). Consider, for example:

Q. Does work bore you, legitimate work?

A. Yeah. If I can't get something that keeps my mind working and keeps me going I can't. . . . I ain't got that good a damn mind, but I mean I've got to keep busy.

Q. And burglary does that for you?

A. Oh, hell yeah. I was having too good a time. I thought this is fun. Hell, the whole town is mine (Tunnell 1992, 63).

Likewise, Malin Akerstrom's work (1985) describes criminals who compare their lifestyles to law-abiders. He reports that 72 percent defined square life as boring and absent of thrills and adventures.

Dannie M. "Red Hog" Martin's essays from prison indicate that he too had little use for work and mainstream society. He viewed both as inferior compared to living the outlaw life within a subculture of other like-minded offenders. Martin claims that his decision to become a criminal and a part of its subculture was just that—a conscious choice. He attributes his decision to one major factor—his lifelong abhorrence for work. Among his essays, he describes watching his grandfather return from the cotton fields, "dirty and tired and getting nowhere." Martin and the people he associated with lived by a simple credo, as he puts it: "That's the line we won't cross: We ain't carryin' no lunch bucket." He goes on to say, as illustration of his disdain for legitimate work:

In my day, it was get a high school education, get a wife, get a bunch of kids, get a tv on credit, get a car and refrigerator on credit. People just sort of drifted through life like that. I never wanted any of it. . . . I rejected the work ethic. If you're lower-class and reject work, there's not much else except crime and prison (Martin and Sussman 1993, 23).

Elsewhere, Dannie Martin, describing his impoverished background and the poor living that his forbearers managed to eke out from their physically demanding jobs, connects this to the development of his own ideology about the meaning of working for a wage:

My forebearers were migrant farm laborers who came to California from the coal mines of Alabama and the pulpwood forests of East Texas in the dust-bowl era of the early '30s. By the time I reached puberty, the idea of work represented to me a twelve-foot cotton sack or a shovel full of heavy mud. My first rebellion was against manual labor (Martin and Sussman 1993, 58).

Property offenders of other studies express similar ideas.

I had seen the way my father was getting the things that he had in life. But, I just wanted things then and there. Like a new car. I couldn't see myself working for two years saving money and then going out and putting it on a car. I wanted my car then and there (Tunnell 1992, 60).

Their inability to locate work and their overwhelming rejection of working for a wage, integrated with their short-term hedonism and need for immediate gratification, are fundamental to the frequency with which they engage in crime, choose their lifestyles, and devote themselves to a subculture.

Immediate gratification is not unique to adult thieves. After all, noncriminals participate in cultures of consumerism that increasingly value the immediacy of fulfilling wants through convenience and providing immediate consumption. From ATMs to pizza deliveries, one-hour shoe repair, photo processing, and prescription lenses, ours is a culture that fosters immediate gratification through convenient and conspicuous consumption. Yet, there are differences in the process. Conventional behavior, for most wage earners, often is a balancing act of deferred and immediate gratification. For conventional consumers, legitimate earnings or credit are necessary requisites to consumption. Working, saving, establishing credit—each represents a deferment of immediate satisfaction. Each also is a pathway by which one ultimately can engage in conspicuous consumption, spontaneous shopping, and other expressive forms of immediate gratification.

Criminals entrenched in a subculture of theft and who reject work or recognize their inability to obtain it, define crime as their sole means for immediate gratification and consumption. Establishing work credentials and credit are not relevant. Consumption and other forms of gratification yield both immediate instrumental and expressive pleasures.

Conspicuous consumption is an important subcultural trait for property offenders. Its value is also socially reproduced within dominant culture. The what and how of socialization into these distinct cultures informs us of the process of gratification through consumption. Instantaneous gratification is important to each. A major distinction is that one group's social experience demands periodic deferment while the other's experience relies on immediacy.

STREET FASHION AND ITS SUBCULTURAL SIGNIFICANCE

Sociology recognizes that subcultures often have their own costuming style. Fashion is a major signifier for affiliation. Yet subcultural fashion is more than simply a way to dress. It is that and more as it becomes the very stuff of the daily lived experiences of subcultural members (Ferrell and Sanders 1995, part 3). Most subcultural members happily conform to the group fashion and style as a reflection of their outward display of association or membership. From bikers to skinheads; from prostitutes to cops; from gang members to Wall Street executives; hippies to punks—each has its own style by which its members are recognized. For example, costuming necessities among bikers include leathers, colors, oil-stained jeans, and tattoos; skinheads display Doc Martens, red suspenders, and shaved hairstyles that give the subculture its name; prostitutes (i.e., streetwalkers) must draw attention to themselves and the services they provide through costuming that most often (among females) includes revealing clothing, high-heeled shoes, particular displays of facial makeup, and posturing; police officers' costuming includes a military-like uniform, a badge, and weapons of force and restraint that project rational legal authority; gang members display their colors, hand signals, and insignias, which differentiate them from other gangs; Wall Street executives dress in expensive Armani business suits, wingtip shoes, white shirts, and power neckties; hippies wear long hair and adorn themselves with patchouli and tie-dyed clothing; and punks wear short hair, body piercings, and Johnny Rotten snarls (Thompson 1967; Hamm 1993; Manning 1997; McKeganey 1996).

Although individuals who do not belong to these illustrative subcultures may occasionally wear such costuming (especially as it becomes co-opted by mainstream fashion industries, for example, as Levis, Doc Martens, and hip-hop clothing have experienced), insiders clothe themselves according to their subcultural norms and as statements of belonging and affiliation. Such dress reflects style and represents their overt displays of subcultural distinctiveness. Style is central to constructing subcultural identities, some of which, such as those among repetitive property offenders, are based on illicit activities (Ferrell 1995).

Although there is no widely recognized costuming specific to adult career criminals, some are committed to clothing themselves in particular fashions as a manifestation of and commitment to criminal street culture or cool (Honaker 1990). Persistent offenders evidently share a commitment to a particular subcultural style. Many property offenders commit crimes to purchase status symbols reflecting their particular association or standing. For example, they will use money from criminal proceeds to buy name-brand clothing to project a certain image that is fundamental to cool street culture and its dress code (Wright and Decker 1994, 43; 1997). By doing this, the intention is to "create an impression of affluence and hipness so that they [will] be admired by their peers on the street and by others" (Wright and Decker 1994, 44).

Race is also a relevant factor to street-centered hipness. Alternative styles and their symbolic meanings differ, to some extent, across races. This perhaps is most obvious among young people who mimic the stylistic presentations of recording artists and professional athletes and seek $100 denims, starter jackets, and the fantastic materialism present in hip-hop videos. Stylistic differences also exist among adult street criminals.

One particular chronic offender, who perhaps is best characterized as a hustler, described his commitment to the subculture of the street in his research interview. He claimed that his stealing progressed from petty activities during his youth to more lucrative and serious crimes during his late teens and early adulthood. His explanation for this modification, though, focuses on the importance assigned to dress, its relevance to projecting a certain image, and its significance for impressing members of the opposite sex. At that stage of his life, in order to dress the part, he simply needed more money. When asked to elaborate on his early involvement in the more lucrative crimes, he responded thus:

> When I started liking girls more or less, dating, and cared about my appearance and the clothes that I wore. I basically needed the money to keep up my standard of living. When I seen my standard of living falling, I had to reinforce it with some currency (Tunnell 1992, 142).

This desire to project a sharply dressed appearance is typical for hustlers, as has been described earlier (Irwin 1970).

Repeat offenders evidently spend their illicit profits on "status-enhancing" items, clothing being foremost among them. Fashion status symbols are widely accepted and propagated among those committed to street crime as a way of life. Posture and costuming congeal into a particular style of street cool imagery "that suggest[s] they [are] members of the aristocracy of the streets" (Wright and Decker 1997, 40). Obvious displays of fashion and style are fundamentally important traits within a street culture that values flaunting eye-catching clothing, from suits to expensive denim; jewelry, from the flashy synthetic to the gaudy gold; vehicles, from sporty cars and SUVs to pickup trucks; and money (when available), conspicuously flashed around and quickly spent. One central benefit of crime as a way of life is to acquire commodities that, when displayed, communicate participation in consuming the latest fashions in clothing, cars, and jewelry (Jacobs and Wright 1999; Mullins and Wright 2003).

Repetitive offenders have few widely recognized compelling features. For example, they possess few resources, they are well known as criminals, and the unsuccessful live under a master status of two-time loser, ex-con, or hood. They are not particularly the best or the brightest, and they have little social capital. Yet, they often disguise these deficiencies with an easily acquired façade of the latest fashions and posturing. Clothes, in their case, do make the man. They believe that this machismo image is at the cutting edge of fashion (at least the fashion that trickles into urban and rural pockets of the United States), and that it exudes coolness and projects independence from social controls, square clothes, and uncool lifestyles. If any one material object can easily transmit cultural attributes, it is clothing in a style, for example, that flaunts street-wise hipness. This transparent cultural artifact is valued and reproduced within subcultures of street criminals.

THE SENSUAL PLEASURES FROM PROPERTY CRIME

Apart from instrumental remuneration, risky decisions, behaviors, and freewheeling lifestyles offer various expressive rewards. These range from sensual thrills and excitement to exhilaration, adrenalin surge, and full-bodied rush. From such disparate behaviors as graffiti writing to skydiving and drug-induced high-speed motorcycle riding to armed robbery, these behaviors involve willing participants operating at the edge that divides sheer pleasure mixed with terror from the consequences of taking things too far

(Ferrell 1993; Lyng 1998; 1990; Thompson 1967; Wright and Decker 1997).

Participating in activities that place actors in dangerous situations while negotiating the boundaries of success and failure has been described as *edgework*. The concept is crucial for understanding risky ventures within which individuals position themselves and where success is determined by stealth, speed, aggression, poise, and determination, all in the face of potential adverse consequences such as injury, imprisonment, and death (Lyng 1990).

For edgework participants, the experience itself rather than its termination generates meaning and pleasure. Like Robert Pirsig's (1974) recollection of edgy and reflective motorcycle experiences, it's the traveling rather than the arriving that draws one to the road. The doctor of journalism, who first put the edge concept to paper, related the experience to high-speed motorcycle driving:

> So the lever goes up into fourth, and now there's no sound except wind. Screw it all the way over, reach through the handlebars to raise the headlight beam, the needle leans down on a hundred, and wind-burned eyeballs strain to see down the centerline, trying to provide a margin for the reflexes. But with the throttle screwed on there is only the barest margin, and no room at all for mistakes . . . and that's when the strange music starts, when you stretch your luck so far that fear becomes exhilaration and vibrates along your arms. . . . The Edge. . . . There is no honest way to explain it because the only people who really know where it is are the ones who have gone over. The others—the living—are those who pushed their control as far as they felt they could handle it, and then pulled back, or slowed down, or did whatever they had to when it came time to choose between Now and Later (Thompson 1965/1990, 111).

This seductive characteristic locates the meaning and dynamics of behavior within the immediacy of the act. The foreground rather than background is all that matters. Regardless of the edgework activity, it involves "a clearly observable threat" that, carried to the extreme, can mean injury or death (Lyng 1990, 857).

Persistent property crime involves risky decisions, behaviors, and lifestyles that place individual offenders and victims in potentially harmful settings with grave consequences. The majority of repetitive property criminals evidently engage in their crimes primarily for economic rewards. This is an undisputed given. But for many, the pleasures, thrills, power, and control are expressive and generate richly sensual meanings for them; for a minority of offenders, these pleasures are more important than financial gain and are the raison d'être for committing crime.

Those who engage in residential burglary as their "main line," for example, oftentimes describe their actions as an occupational choice and an event that contains its own seductive properties. These edge-working burglars report that they do not "typically commit burglaries as much for the money as for the psychic rewards" (Wright and Decker 1994, 56). They burglarize homes primarily because they enjoy it and benefit from "the risks and challenges inherent in the crime" (Wright and Decker 1994, 56). Consider the words of the following high-rate residential burglar who used simple brute force to gain entry.

> If I had to write a damn paper on the reason I steal, there would be one sentence—it was for the game. It's a high. Now, I mean it's exhilarating. I mean, some people like racquetball and some people like tennis, but I get off going through doors (Tunnell 1992, 45).

His game playing was reward enough as he negotiated the dangers of dropping off the edge and staying a step and a burglary ahead of the authorities.

This burglar's behavior and the meaning associated with it are also indicative of rebellion. The rebelliousness itself is a form of edgework, for rebellion nearly always notifies the authorities of one's existence, actions, and posture. Taking such positions is a warning, a rebel yell that a stand is being made, for right or wrong. As long as one can walk the edge, not fall off, or be tripped up by the authorities, risky behavior delivers sheer pleasure.

There are few legitimate activities for accomplished burglars, and even fewer provide such internal satisfaction. In their opinion, crime is their only option. One individual, for example, who almost daily engaged in shoplifting, described the enjoyment of his craft and the pleasures derived from the act itself:

> I enjoyed it and the people with me enjoyed it. It's exciting to do it. Wanting to do it, man. Wanting to do it. Love to do it. Love to do it would be the word (Tunnell 1992, 44).

However, the thrill of the work is often not enough. In those cases, edgeworkers artificially inflate the risks of their work to generate greater exhilaration, thrill, or rush. Consider the following words from a chronic shoplifter:

> A. I'm the type of person, man, if I could steal something from way in the back row or if the store manager is standing here and I could take something right under his nose, that's what I'd get.

Q. Why would you prefer that?

A. Because it's more of an accomplishment (Tunnell 1992, 44).

Offenders oftentimes envision themselves as adventurers who derive an experiential "feeling of being closer to real life and experiencing 'more'" than they believe is ever generated from legal activities (Akerstrom 1993, 27). They see themselves as "really having lived and having experienced, as opposed to ordinary people." Such offenders are living proof of the social-psychological meaning derived from committing property crimes. This satisfaction is derived in part from the thrill or rush of doing edgework, such as burglary, shoplifting, or armed robbery, and has been reported in first-hand accounts by a variety of offenders (Frazier and Meisenhelder 1985). Such satisfactions also are relevant to offenders' commitment to living a relatively autonomous lifestyle.

Armed robbery, the property crime that implicitly and necessarily contains and depends on the threat of violence, also provides seductive psychic rewards. It is a risky activity that generates satisfaction. The derived pleasure or "rush" is dependent, in part, on instilling fear in and exercising control over victims. Consider, for example, these declarations:

> The money is the point of robbery, that's all. But pulling the gun, watching their face, how scared they get and all . . . that's fun too.

> This might sound stupid, but I also like to see a person get scared, be scared of the pistol. You got power. I come in here with a big old pistol and I ain't playing. You gonna do what I say. I like robbery cause you got the power . . . (Wright and Decker 1997, 56).

Making money from robbery and the act itself, with all its sensual attractions, is revealed in the following interview:

> A. It's a surprise, an element of surprise. You go in and you throw a gun on the table and everybody just flips out. But it never did scare me because I always just put myself in their position. But it's just getting in that door. After you get through that door it ain't nothing, it's like you're running, like you own the place.
>
> Q. You said like you own the place?
>
> A. Yeah, you are ruling everything because everybody, whoever is in there, is going to pay attention to you. I didn't want to hurt nobody. The only thing I wanted was the money. If you go in there you've got to play that act all the way out whether you get hurt or not.
>
> Q. I think you're saying you were also prepared to do whatever to get the money?

A. Right. It wouldn't be that they'd try to harm me, it would be that
they wouldn't give up the money. Because, you see, if you go in there
and then let them tell you what to do, then there ain't no sense in you
going in there at all (Tunnell 1992, 50).

These men are powerless within every other situation that they experience (except perhaps in sexually dominating women). Yet crime, as edgework that contains seductive properties, places them on the boundary between order and disorder as they create and impose their own order on
situations and individuals over which they otherwise have no control. Residential burglars, for example, negotiate the unknown, the unforeseen, and
the what-might-happen-next scenario inside strange and unfamiliar houses
with little knowledge of their victims, their location, or when they might
return home. Robbers impose their power over others while doing their
best to prevent sudden and violent disorderliness. Robbery is a momentary
exhilaration where offenders are in ultimate and final control. They negotiate the tensions of containing victims, instilling fear, and getting money, all
while consciously and enjoyably operating at the edge.

As offenders negotiate the variables necessary for successfully committing a crime, they, like individuals involved in noncriminal edgework, experience nervousness or "butterflies" beforehand. Yet, as they carry out their
crimes, the nervousness rescinds and their uneasiness transforms into an intense, focused self-determination that is ultimately pleasurable (Lyng 1990,
860). The following words of an accomplished armed robber, for example,
indicate his focused attention on successfully completing his work:

When I walked in the place I really didn't think nothing. I mean it was
just like my mind was blank when I walked in. I knowed what I was in
there for (Tunnell 1992, 81).

Others compared the nervousness they experienced before a crime to
that of musicians before a performance; in both cases, they vanish once the
work begins (Private interview 1987). As edgeworkers begin to mediate the
tensions between nervousness, completing the task at hand, and maintaining control of the situation, they come to define their own expertise and
abilities as those personal features that account for their success.

Specific skills are fundamental to edgework, whether it is legal, illegal,
or somewhere in between. Robbers and burglars, like skydivers, bridge
jumpers, and stock car racers, possess and use skills specific to their occupation. Stealth, speed, strength, aggression, mental toughness, the ability to in-
still fear and paralyze victims, and the acumen for dealing with fences, drug

dealers, and legal authorities all constitute those necessary traits of successfully maintaining a criminal career. Criminals tend to view these performance assets as requisites necessary for completing the crime and for containing unanticipated dangers. Furthermore, these traits are viewed as necessary for surviving those unexpected hazards, such as when homeowners
return during a burglary or when an armed robbery victim resists or produces a weapon. These unexpected risks would likely result in failure, injury, or death among the inexperienced who does not possess such career
requisites. Yet, they are successfully negotiated by experienced and seasoned
property offenders. Although the threat of violence is a feature of armed
robbery, fortunately only 3 percent of victims' injuries result in hospitaliza-
tion (Karmen 1995, chap. 2).

Beyond these sensual pleasures derived from crime, some persistent offenders, at least occasionally, commit crimes for revenge. These motivated acts
provide a pleasant or at least satisfied feeling. For example, Paul Cromwell et al.
(1991, 22) report "about 30 percent of the informants reported committing at
least one burglary for revenge." Revenge provides a sense of evening the score
even during those times when the victim is not necessarily the individual who
wronged the property offender. Some offenders, for example, strike out at a
generalized "other" as a symbol of the party that they believe did them wrong
(Tunnell 1992; Wright and Decker 1997). One career offender interviewed
claimed, for example, that after his first incarceration at a young age, he was
outraged at society. Most of his criminal actions afterward consisted of striking
out at a generalized other or any representation of legitimate social order as a
means of retaliating against the police, the man, or authority. He had decided
to "get those sons-of-bitches," meaning the police and prosecutors, yet his actions materialized into attacking people (and their property) who were imma-
terial to his incarceration (Private interview 1988). Nonetheless, he obtained
some pleasure from his crimes of revenge.

Crime clearly has multiple meanings to criminal actors and its significance is relevant to those who habitually commit property crime. Understanding the meanings attributed to crime implies confronting its foreground—the immediacy of the event, the seduction that draws one into the
activity itself, and the pleasures and sensations derived from it (Katz 1988).
These foreground attributes are of such importance to criminals' continued
participation in illegalities that beyond these "moral and sensual attractions
in doing evil" there are few logical explanations (Katz 1988, 218).

The expressive rewards enjoyed by property offenders are not solely
individually based, social-psychological phenomena. They are culturally
shaped and bounded by and within the powerless, thrill-seeking, bad-assed,

underclass individuals who embrace thrills as interruptions to an otherwise monotonous existence. These individuals come to view their crimes as far more compelling than any excitement ever generated from straight lifestyles and dominant cultural activities.

The subcultural trait of thrill-seeking is indicative of edgework as a hyperreality; it is a vastly different experience from normal social life that for edgeworkers is a dreary reality (Lyng 1990, 880). Although the importance of these rewards varies, they nonetheless are fundamental to property criminal subcultures. They are created within and reproduced by group members and are vastly different from those central to and reproduced by dominant culture or other subcultures.

DRUG ABUSE, CULTURE, AND LIFESTYLE

The dysfunctional effects of drug abuse and their relationship to crime have been recognized in the United States since the mid-eighteenth century and are "well ingrained in the American experience" (Walters 1994, vii). Among individuals deeply entrenched in street and criminal subcultures, drug and alcohol abuse are nearly universal features. Substance abuse is an activity of social importance and indicative of subcultural identity.

Among individuals whose drug and alcohol use becomes a pervasive addiction, use is transformed from its original liberating and socially developed meaning into constricting, socially isolating, and dysfunctional behaviors. Addiction itself generates its own particular meanings. With addiction, taking drugs becomes a necessity. Thus, rather than providing pleasure, as the effects of drugs are described among casual users, drug use among addicts becomes a pain-avoidance process where regular and frequent dosages are necessitated by the ever-threatening pain from withdrawal symptoms. Alfred Lindesmith (1968, 8) describes this process and resulting condition:

> The critical experience in the fixation process is not the positive euphoria produced by the drug but rather the relief of the pain that invariably appears when a physically dependent person stops using the drug. . . . The individual not only must experience relief of withdrawal distress but must understand or conceptualize this experience in a particular way. He must realize that his distress is produced by the interruption of prior regular use of the drug.

In other words, there is an interactive learning process specific to drug use and to becoming a drug user. There is also a process to drug abuse and to becoming an addict. This includes learning to recognize traits characteristic of withdrawal and relating those to the relief derived from the additional medicalization of symptoms. These are social processes that are based on interaction and that enable the construction of definitions favorable to drug use and to actions that satisfy addictions.

Doubts are expressed occasionally about the relevance of drug abuse and addiction to crime. From several studies, we know that the addiction itself (especially among the dispossessed lower class) typically necessitates frequent participation in criminal activity. These crimes most often produce minimal financial payoffs (e.g., only a few hundred dollars at best). Few alternative behaviors are possible.[1] Treated as dubious by some, this addiction-crime relationship is both physiological and social-psychological. Furthermore, withdrawal from a drug includes both physiological and psychological dimensions. As long as underclass addicts insist on avoiding the painful symptoms of doing without their drug, crime will remain a viable source of revenue and will likely increase with the frequency and urgency of withdrawal symptoms. Whereas drug use during the early stages of an addict's experiences produces pleasurable sensations, as time goes by its increasingly central function becomes one of pain avoidance or withdrawal. In other words, an addict continues using the drug "to avoid the symptoms which he knows will appear if he stops using it" (Lindesmith 1968, 32).

Lindesmith's unparalleled work logically traces the development of drug addiction through delineations of pre-addicted states, the addictive state, addicts' tendency to increase dosages, and the centrality of the pains of withdrawal to ongoing addictions. Addiction is said to begin when users first experience, accurately identify, and attempt to alleviate withdrawal symptoms produced by physical dependencies (Becker 1963). Addiction, therefore, is not simply an inherent property of a drug's pharmacological action. It is also something other than the recognition of physical dependence marked by relief from withdrawal symptoms. It is this and more as it takes shape and develops meaning through a learning process in a situation of social interaction. The process is one of physiological cause-and-effect relationships perceptually constructed by users and typically within drug-abusing subcultures. The repetition of relief from withdrawal and the recognition of the relationship results in addiction (Lindesmith 1968, 73; see also Akers 1998; 1991).

Addiction, though, is not a linear inevitability but rather results as individuals regularly and frequently use (in one form or another) addictive drugs within social groups and subcultures condoning drug use. This social and casual use is just that—use. Dependency is not yet an issue. In this pre-addiction stage, withdrawal symptoms are not yet a dominant force in users' lives and do not manifest themselves as motivation for acting. Instead, drug use continues for various reasons—as rebellion, retreat, pleasure, a manifestation of a cultural trait within subcultures—that are vastly different from drug use and explanations for using after addiction is established.

Drug use, especially within subcultures, is an activity that is similar to those described in the previous section—edgework. Prior to dysfunctional addiction, drug use for edgeworkers represents fun, free-spirited, altered states. The act of taking drugs and the subculturally defined pleasures from them are relevant to thrill-seeking individuals who live to love and love to live on the edge. Regardless of the original intentions among casual drug users or those who use as a part of their ongoing commitment to edgework, addiction may result from any continued and regular use (Lindesmith 1968, 83-84).

As individuals use regularly and develop drug dependencies, they often increase their dosages beyond what is needed to simply sustain addictions. The dosage necessary to maintain addiction, or the "comfort dose," is the amount that provides a consistent level of intoxication (which, of course, implies pain avoidance). But a second dosage type, an additional amount which users define as essential to their comfort, the "deluxe dose," manifests itself in unnecessary expense and troubles (e.g., making connections, acquiring money, committing other crimes) and represents "a psychological rather than a physiological need" (Lindesmith 1968, 90). Addicts' earliest experiences with withdrawal symptoms oftentimes result in the tendency to magnify their importance and immediacy. In order to avoid withdrawals and feeling trapped, addicts may throw caution to the wind and increase dosages in an effort to prevent the likelihood of repeating the painful experience (Lindesmith 1968, 91). Working against this tendency to overuse drugs clearly involves ongoing exercises in self-control. This new definition of their situation and one that stays the course toward addiction is fundamentally relevant to large numbers of repetitive property offenders. Their dependence on the deluxe dose demands regular cash expenditures that are made possible almost solely by ongoing and frequent participation in property crime.

Nonetheless, the drug-crime relationship remains the subject of intense debate and research. Studies about this relationship have produced differing results, namely: (1) drug use leads to criminal participation; (2) involvement in crime leads to drug use; (3) the criminalization of drugs causes crime; and (4) the relationship between drug use and crime is spurious (Brownfield 1996, 128; Gentry 1995). The literature on drug addiction and criminal activity is abundant. From this body of literature, we know that addictive narcotic use is strongly related to criminal behavior. Research shows that the overwhelming majority of people involved in crimes began their addictive careers before the initiation of their criminal careers (speaking to the first point above). However, causality cannot be inferred from this since research also shows involvement in crime oftentimes precedes drug use. In fact, predatory offenders begin their drug careers earlier than most but typically after their first involvement with crime (addressing the second point above). Those whose criminal activity precedes their drug addiction are at a greater risk of engaging solely in predatory crimes (Farabee, Joshi, and Anglin 2001). Research also shows that the rate at which individuals engage in crime during periods of drug use "may be as much as five times the rate during periods of non-use of narcotics" (Brownfield 1996, 129). Such findings (related to the third point above) speak to the frequency of crime commission during periods of drug addiction, propelled in part by the criminalization of drugs and their resulting inflated prices. Drug use or abuse may not cause crime, but for those with few resources at their disposal and who are entrenched within a culture supporting illicit activities, participation in crime intensifies with escalating drug use. Offenders must frequently generate sufficient income to support ongoing addictions. In other words, although drug use is not a cause of property crime, "drug use may be viewed as a multiplier of existing criminologic predisposition" (Brownfield 1996, 131).[2]

Drug use among offenders (among both the unsuccessful, who have been the subject of most research, and the successful) is widespread. The National Institute of Justice (1996) survey research of 20,737 adult males who were arrested and booked in twenty-three metropolitan areas shows that at every site, a majority tested positive for drugs, with cocaine dominating. Given the limitations of these data, those arrested with drugs in their system cannot be differentiated from those with ongoing addictions.

Other recent aggregate data also show that the number of crimes committed by individuals under the influence of a drug has increased significantly. From 1986 to 1991, the percentage of prisoners who regularly used cocaine increased from 22 to 36 percent. Among individuals arrested and tested for drugs, positive results varied across twenty-four U.S. cities from 47 percent (in Phoenix) to 78 percent (in Philadelphia) (DiMascio 1995, 27). Clearly, drug use is widespread among those engaged in crimes. Department of Justice data from 1997 show that 57 percent of state prisoners and 45 percent of federal prisoners claimed to have used drugs in the month before their offense—an increase from 50 percent and 32 percent respectively from a 1991 report. Likewise, increases occurred during the same period for those who claimed to have committed their crimes while under the influence of a drug. In 1991, 31 percent of state and 17 percent of federal prisoners made this claim, while in 1997, 33 percent of state and 22 percent of federal inmates did.

Alcohol is also widely used among those engaged in criminal behavior. Recent data indicate that 38 percent of those in state prisons and 20 percent of those in federal prisons were drinking when they committed the crime. About three-quarters of all prisoners are characterized by the Justice Department as being involved with alcohol or drug *abuse* in the time leading up to their arrest (More than three-quarters of prisoners had abused drugs in the past [1999]). As the remainder of this section shows, drug addiction, especially among those who frequently engage in the most serious property crimes—burglary and armed robbery—is a central feature of active street criminal subcultures.

Although the nature of the association remains unclear, evidence of a drug-crime relationship emerges from both self-reported and official data. From the seemingly disparate hypotheses, an inclusive and parsimonious lifestyle theory has emerged. It suggests that drug abuse and persistent criminality represent interrelated lifestyles (Walters 1994, 6). This explanation fundamentally is subcultural with a focus on deviant lifestyles at its center, comprised of various conditionings, choices, and changes across time and careers. Regarding conditions, those most telling personal and situational variables that account for one's participation in drug use and criminal activity are age, poverty and social class, and peer relations. And regarding one's first experimentation with drugs, research shows some overlap with other delinquent activities, especially during adolescence, when peer pressure and influence are perhaps at their most intense (Walters 1994, 20).

Drug use and criminal participation are part of a broader personal and social orientation or lifestyle perspective that also focuses on the interaction of personal choice, structural antecedents, and situational settings (Walters 1994; Felson 1994; Wright and Decker 1994; 1997). Central to its explanations for criminal participation are both back- and foreground factors. Criminal behavior and drug abuse are "conceptualized as overlapping lifestyles that, although distinct, are nonetheless bound by a common set of current-contextual conditions, choices, cognitions, and change strategies" (Walters 1994, 95–96). These commonalities are especially relevant to repetitive property offenders whose crime commission changes as their drug problems escalate and as their addictions vary across time.

Street criminals share a common lifestyle as reported in numerous studies. Nearly five decades ago, Walter Miller (1958) described commonalities pertinent to lower-class culture and referred to them as *focal concerns*.

More recently, Miller's focal concerns (although this term was not used) have been applied to repeat property offenders who manifest specific characteristics that differentiate them from others. In particular, those most active and persistent offenders tend "to get into all kinds of trouble, criminal or not" (Felson 1994, 19). This emphasis on "trouble" hearkens a return to Miller's focal concerns or life themes, which are determined by and reflective of lower-class culture, a distinct subculture effected by structural constraints and shaped by limitations and separateness.

From the various empirical studies with repetitive property offenders, we find that drugs and crime are intimately interrelated within a larger criminal-underclass subculture and lifestyle. Today, Miller may agree, that drug use and abuse represents another focal concern (or one that is subsumed within his concepts—trouble and excitement).

Among one sample of property offenders who reported needing money for drugs, only 10 percent stated that they would continue committing crimes if their financial needs, including money for drugs, were satisfied (Reppetto 1974, 22)—clearly a drug-crime self-reported relationship. Research with thirty burglars likewise revealed that each had an ongoing drug addiction, most commonly to heroin and cocaine; their offending frequency was linked to swings in their addictions and their immediate need for cash (Cromwell et al. 1991, 15).

By examining addictions and the importance assigned to drug use within criminal subcultures, Rengert and Wasilchick (1985, 54) discovered that the property offenders in their sample needed money both for drugs and expressive needs rather than sustenance per se. Likewise, Cromwell et al. (1991, 21) reported that, other than cash to support drug addictions, their burglars desired money "for the activity they loosely labeled as partying . . . [and] to maintain a fast expensive life." This is consistent with Miller (1958) and the more recent research of Wright and Decker (1994; 1997), who describe their offenders as entrenched within the excitement and immediacy of street culture, including drug cultures.

Other research using unincarcerated, active burglars reports "that the percentage of drug-using burglars is much greater than that reported in prior studies" (Cromwell et al. 1991, 53). Research also indicates that the link between drug use and criminal behavior is a positive one since increases in drug use are related to an intensification of criminal activity. This results in a life of escalating street crime and drug abuse, leaving the possibility of employment increasingly difficult to locate or maintain. Individuals in this situation are "often dropped out of legitimate society" and maintain their drug habits "through full-time criminal activity. Because drug users must establish and maintain illicit contacts in order to buy drugs, they are drawn further into a network of criminal associates, and thus more deeply into a deviant life-style" (Cromwell et al. 1991, 54). This is relevant to the lifestyle approach and to the hypothesis that persistent drug use (and addiction) propels individuals without other means further into frequent crime commission and further entrenchment in subcultures with focal concerns of crime and drug use. In fact, most burglars report that they would not commit crime if not for their drug addiction, or, at the least, their frequency of burglaries would decline (Cromwell et al. 1991, 55; Reppetto 1974, 72).

Addicts interviewed by various researchers refer to property crimes as their occupation or work, meaning that it is their main line for getting money to buy drugs. "Rico, a heroin addict, said: 'I think of this as work just like you think of your job as work. You are a professor, I'm a junkie and a burglar'" (Cromwell et al. 1991, 56). This is strikingly similar to stories reported in other research, such as when a highly active armed robber related his work to that of the researcher's.

> I know that I'm doing wrong and I'm taking a chance. It's the same way that you got in your car and you started down here. Right? What would have happened if you started thinking, "Well, look here, I could have a car wreck around this next corner here?" Are you going to turn around and go back? It's your job to get here and do that, right? It's the same thing. It's a job to me, so I do my best at it (Tunnell 1992, 110).

Floyd Feeney (1986, 58) reports that among his sample of 113 armed robbers characterized as poor, 60 percent said they robbed for money, and nearly a third of those, most of whom were heroin addicts, robbed for money for drugs. Wright and Decker's (1994, 41) interview research with active burglars also shows that many of their participants committed burglaries "solely for the purpose of obtaining money to buy drugs." Drug-addicted offenders, "experience considerable pressure to continue, even if this involves breaking the law" (Wright and Decker 1994, 39).

Some offenders who use up their drugs during "partying" immediately go out and burgle to maintain the frivolity. Some recent work has focused on offenders' insistence on keeping the party going rather than on their physiological addictions or on the meanings they give to use or abuse drugs. "Life as party" and "keeping the party going" convey explanations different from those that focus on drug addiction. Rather, these descriptions characterize individuals as, for example, hedonistic and shortsighted. Yet, these traits and social activities are best appreciated when recognizing their subcultural importance and the relevance attached to these activities by the subcultural members. Keeping the party going, and especially the kinds of parties described in the literature (e.g., using drugs, drinking to excess), is likely a subcultural trait. This characteristic is important especially within criminal subcultures (and some college fraternity subcultures).

Within criminal subcultures, these behaviors are culturally constructed and reproduced. They are used as identifying characteristics of the subcultural members and likely are a part of Miller's "excitement" focal concern. Keeping the party going is a subcultural style. The types of drugs, the frequency of their use, and the means by which they are obtained reflect subcultural style (Mullins and Wright 2003). Yet, within criminal or addict subcultures, these activities, containing life and death meanings, emerge, take hold, and become socially reproduced. After all, nearly everyone—criminal and noncriminal—enjoys keeping the party going, whether that means opening another bottle of wine, staying up a little later, pouring another shot of whiskey, or having one more dance. Offenders are distinguished from nonoffenders by their class and culture—class-based limitations and cultural acceptances of crime as the means by which to keep the party going and as a means of minimizing the pain of withdrawal—whether real or imagined and whether physiological or psychological.

Although offenders may exaggerate their commitment to crime and drug use, the significance of drug addiction to frequent and repetitive property crime commission cannot be overstated. But, whether physiological or psychological, offenders define their addictions as real with consequences that represent harsh reality (e.g., from withdrawal pain to arrest). Drug use may explain little about the etiology of crime, but it is fundamental to understanding the frequency of crime commission, individuals' ongoing criminal participation, the duration of criminal careers, and the cultures of chronic offenders.

AUTONOMY

Repetitive property offenders enjoy unfettered and autonomous lives. They embrace few responsibilities and commitments. And those obligations that they do take on often go ignored and remain unfulfilled. Their commitment to living autonomous, free-spirited, nomadic lives is manifest in a number of activities and worldviews. For example, they proudly exhibit an ongoing aversion to legitimate work, they largely reject hierarchical strictures, even among their criminal cohort, and they consider their adventurous, unrestrained behaviors as qualitatively superior to restricted, square lifestyles.

Autonomy represents, among other cultural traits, a focal concern or life theme and was first described by Miller (1958) in his explications of distinct lower-class subcultures. Autonomy for Miller is two-edged. On one hand, lower-class individuals, entrenched in their own class-bound subculture, evade controls on their lives. For example, they verbally insist that no one's going to push them around. On the other hand, while rejecting various cultural controls, lower-class individuals inevitably gravitate toward some restrictions on their lives. They then live within structured, routinized environments. The lives of repeat property offenders typically range between freedom and independent, income-generating ventures to an almost complete loss of autonomy. For example, their independence is interrupted when they are removed from their free-spirited street existence and placed under the watchful custody of the criminal justice system.

Repeat offenders, who display a commitment to autonomy as a subcultural trait, often drift from the controlling forces of total institutions to free-spirited, independent ventures. Reminiscent of Miller, Martin observes,

> One day [convicts] are shoved into a real cage, and the iron doors slam shut behind them. The most common look in their eyes at the moment the last door clanks firmly shut is a strange mixture of resignation and relief. Suddenly they are able to handle their habits and to get a grip on their lives. The choice isn't theirs anymore. Jail restores order and certainty in a person's life. Meals are served according to a rigid schedule, laundry exchanged at definite times; sick call, mail call, and visits are all at fixed hours on designated days. We can't see out the windows of the jail, but we see the future stretched before us in a rigid, orderly fashion. From lives of chaos, uncertainty, and danger, we are thrust into order, security, and boredom (Martin and Sussman 1993, 81).

Autonomy is important for understanding the activities of repetitive criminals. It is a manifestation of both their class and culture.

Miller's (1958) primary focus is on divergent cultures—dominant cultures and subcultures—that undoubtedly share some similarities but also exhibit vastly different norms, values, and lifestyles. For Miller, there exists an identifiable and distinct culture—the lower class—whose impact, when compared to dominant, middle-class culture, is more pronounced in socializing its members. A life of poverty is marked by a gradual socialization into a lower-class subculture that persists and is socially reproduced. This is especially the case with homogenous and socially (and at times, geographically) isolated subcultures.

The primary social force that keeps these cultures separate is *class*. The resulting class-bound social values and ways of life are constructions of the distinct subcultures. Subcultural members typically live marginally to the dominant cultural-economic system and rarely experience success in legitimate social and legal realms. For Miller, the lower class simply develops its own unique culture with its own unique identity, ways of life, norms, and values that are qualitatively different from dominant middle-class culture. This subculture, a feature of lower-class communities, "exerts the most direct influence on behavior" (Miller 1958, 5–6). It is the conflict between the subculture and the dominate culture, each exerting powerful forces on individuals, that explains behavior defined as deviant, inappropriate, violent, and criminal (e.g., Chambliss 1973).

Male role-development within the subculture depends largely on conforming to cultural expectations, behaviors, life themes, and focal concerns. Males socialized into this subculture develop behavior that is acceptable in lower-class subcultures while in conflict with the dominant one. Males commit "a high degree of emotional involvement" to these concerns as part of their socialization into and entrenchment within this distinctive subculture (Miller 1958, 6). Since these focal concerns are potentially criminogenic, crime is a relatively commonplace result of social interaction and a normal behavioral response (Tunnell and Cox 1995, 379–80).[3] For example, overt displays of criminal cool, independence, or simply hanging out are "attractive in comparison to other pursuits that their lives have to offer" (Honaker 1990, 50). Posturing of this sort often leads to other socially acceptable forms of deviance that are supported by normative subcultural values.

Property offenders' commitment to autonomy and their rejection of the controlling effects of employment are well illustrated in the film *Raising Arizona*. During one scene, Edwina (portrayed by Holly Hunter) announces that the struggling-to-reform ex-con (portrayed by Nicholas Cage) is looking for work. A young prison escapee poses the culturally relevant question to him: "You're young and got your health. What the hell do you want with a job?"

Autonomy, an ongoing life theme within lower-class, criminal subcultures, is manifest daily as males wander about as urban nomads. Time is spent drifting across their *home range*, or "some bounded geographic territory within which an individual characteristically circulates in the course of carrying out daily life-rounds" (Stein and McCall 1994, 77). Although a term first applied to the homeless, a roaming lifestyle is typical of the myriad street criminals who drift from one place to another for sleep, sex, or drugs, and who maintain a constant hustle and a watchful eye for criminal opportunities (Tunnell 1992, 140–45). As they make their rounds, the routes used by street criminals overlap and form some semblance of a community of thieves, armed robbers, drug dealers, hustlers, buyers and sellers of stolen goods, prostitutes, and victims. Criminals' attachment to autonomy and involvement in street culture is manifest in such activities as roaming from one temporary dwelling to another, moving from one girlfriend to another, hanging out, fulfilling immediate wants, and drifting through alienated alleys and impoverished inner-city neighborhoods characterized by their predatory violence, drugs, hustles, and street corner prostitution (Wright and Decker 1997, 37). This urban, nomadic, subcultural lifestyle may be one of autonomy and free-spiritedness, yet it is also within loose and distrustful subcultural communities (Stein and McCall 1994).[4] Of course, rural and small town offenders do not roam alleys and city streets. They, unlike their urban counterparts, are dependent on the automobile. Their familiar terrain consists of unimproved and county back roads that join highways or a web of other rural roads (see, e.g., Weisheit et al. 1999, chap. 2). These are the areas where rural offenders feel comfortable and with which they are well acquainted. Drifting into the city to commit crime is as foreign to them as urban offenders venturing into the suburbs. Each has its familiar terrain or awareness space.

Whether urban or rural, the positive returns from offenders' edgework, their autonomous, free-spirited, street-centered daily living, coupled with subcultural acceptance of and support for these traits, may account, in part, for their long-term commitment to a life of crime even when interrupted by capture or a stint in prison.

GENDER, MASCULINITIES, AND SEXISM

Public masculinity, as formation and manifestation of gender, is also relevant to male offenders, their ongoing aggressiveness, their public displays of bad-assed behaviors, and the macho style embedded in their criminal subcultures. Among male offenders who are repetitively engaged in property crimes, their constructions of public masculinity seem to be widespread and are inseparable from their ongoing hedonistic, autonomous, trouble-filled lives. Given the extent of some males' disreputable actions, their illegal, aggressive, and violent behaviors perhaps "should be viewed as *normal* rather than unusual or abnormal" (Newburn and Stanko 1994, 3–4).

Furthermore, men's behavior arguably is best understood within a context of differential power relations based on gender, public expressions, and ongoing constructions of public masculinities. After all, social science has known for decades which groups commit the vast majority of property, violent, and corporate crime. No matter the data source—arrest, self-reporting, or victimization—each indicates that males, young and old, commit more conventional and serious crimes than do women and girls (Chesney-Lind and Paramore 2001).

Criminology has consistently claimed that gender is "the strongest predictor of criminal involvement" (Messerschmidt 1993, 1), yet criminology has not adequately included women into the research enterprise. It has both ignored and devalued them, their illicit activities, and, to a large extent, their victimization. When displaying the same behaviors as males, females generally have been misrepresented in criminology's attempt to understand gendered crime. As a result, the ongoing allegation, that criminological theories explain male rather than human behavior, seems valid (Messerschmidt 1993, 13).

Focusing almost solely on men and boys, criminological theory and most research have perhaps given too little attention to their gendered behaviors and their constructions. Sociology has attempted to account for male domination of criminal activities. But critics allege that most academic work in this area eventually returns, at least in part, to biological differences rather than post-feminist explanations of gendered activities and the masculinities that males internalize and display (Messerschmidt 1993, 27).

Related to masculinities and gender, the literature on persistent property offenders shows that they are a sexist lot. Sexism runs rampant amid their subcultures, which historically and currently exclude women. Ostracism of females is firmly entrenched in this male-dominated culture, and it has become effectually institutionalized. For example, Darryl Steffensmeier and Robert Terry (1986, 304) interviewed forty-nine male property offenders, some of whom were "career thieves," who displayed attitudes that restricted women from participating in the criminal underworld. These offenders' dominant beliefs about women were that they are "physically weaker, more emotional, less reliable, and as not having enough daring and endurance to make it in crime." In other words, according to male criminals, women lack those very qualities central to crimes of theft. Such unfavorable definitions of women apparently "provide considerable justification for the exclusion of females from criminal participation" (Steffensmeier and Terry 1986, 315). Although male offenders commit crimes that include women, the latter's involvement typically is "sporadic and situational—an occasional occurrence" rather than indicative of ongoing partnerships (Steffensmeier and Terry 1986, 306).

The exclusion of women in crime is culturally institutionalized and contains structurally based limits on the range of illegal opportunities available to females. The entrenched sexism is explained as a link between structure and agency. There arguably is a "*collective* and *cumulative* side" to males' opposition to females' participation, especially in the more lucrative and menacing property crimes. "As crime becomes organized, through increasing degrees of informal to formal organization, male opposition is likely to have contextual or *structural effects* which extend far beyond individual personalities" (Steffensmeier and Terry 1986, 320, emphasis in original). As a result, male criminal subcultures assume specific institutionalized forms that are culturally reproduced.

Beyond the structural and institutionalized features of sexism and exclusion, male property offenders, in a variety of qualitative studies, have given their personal reasons for excluding women. Their explanations, however, reflect the subculturally entrenched devaluing of women that dominates male criminality (see, e.g., Bowker 1998). For example, in the following passage, an armed robber offered his thoughts on his crimes and on the value of intimidation, which he believes is fundamental to this crime type:

> Maybe now if women know more about weapons and that, they'd be of more use. But, I don't think they'd be taken seriously, know what I mean? (Steffensmeier and Terry 1986, 310)

And the following words from two different male offenders clearly indicate their refusal to participate in crimes with women and display blatantly sexist attitudes:

> I don't know why I wouldn't work with women. I guess there's reasons for it. It seems to me that maybe they're just not put together for it, you know what I mean? I don't know if I'm old fashioned or what but I don't think you'd want to be using women for crime and that, do you?
>
> Why wouldn't I use a woman? Well, because I'm from the old school. And the old school says a woman is in her place at home and that's where she should be and not participating in burglaries and criminal activities.
> I just don't see having a woman do crimes. Her place is in bed and in the kitchen I guess (Steffensmeier and Terry 1986, 314).

Recent research shows that the same ideology, culturally entrenched and reproduced, continues. Patriarchal attitudes and behaviors, among males who live off crime, frame the initiation and participation in burglary. Continued research with male and (the few) female burglars shows that both are first initiated into crime by their intimate others. Females are initiated into crime by males (and not vice versa). Males and females recognize that burglary and other street crimes are masculine activities. Residential burglary in particular (much like armed robbery) is a gender-stratified offense (Mullins and Wright 2003).

With such wide recognition and institutionalized exclusion, illegitimate opportunities remain differentially distributed (Cloward and Ohlin 1960). This, of course, has been the case with legitimate opportunity structures. Sexism and exclusion by gender remain deeply entrenched in illicit opportunity structures as well. Rather than relying on law and politics to preserve men's privileged position, those within criminal subcultures depend on tradition, socialization, overt sexism, hostility, violence, and intimidation to preserve the gendered arena of predatory criminal behavior.

CONCLUSION

Women remain culturally excluded from both legitimate and illegitimate occupations. As much as women are left out of the illicit actions of the street (with prostitution the primary exception), they are excluded even more so from illegalities made possible through legal occupations—white-collar crime. In both street and suite crime, women are excluded from participating through entrenched subcultural norms and values that reflect institutionalized sexism no matter whether it is illegitimate or legitimate, blue collar or white-collar work. Opportunity, a central variable for the occurrence of any crime, is simply not as readily available to women as men, and, as the evidence continues to show, such differential access is not a naturally occurring phenomenon. Rather, it is, in part, a product of male-dominated cultures of both the official world and the various criminal enterprises within underground economies and criminal subcultures.

In both crime types, street or suite, class may not be as relevant as culture and, arguably, the dominant one—a culture of consumer-driven materialism and competitiveness. We can only speculate about the number of individuals who remain unaffected by a culture of competition; however, such cultural traits have been proven to be widely and happily accepted and reproduced. The relevance of crime as spirited competition varies across subcultures, from endorsement and participation in it to outright condemnation of it.

Class remains relevant to criminal behavior on at least two grounds. First, it determines opportunity. Second, the class with the fewest opportunities—the poor—has members that engage in behaviors that are treated as the most immediately threatening to property and person.

The meaning of crime for the lawbreaker lies in both the foreground and background. Criminal behavior, perhaps set in motion and restricted in choice by background factors, comes to life and takes on relevant meaning, identity, and daily existence within the foreground. That meaning, those identities, and those daily existences are carved from both class location and cultural peculiarities.

NOTES

1. It probably goes without saying that addicted individuals who earn a decent legitimate wage are able to acquire drugs without engaging in further crime, unlike addicts who are poor, committed to street culture, and who have little social capital.

2. However, as most criminology remains "malestream," we should be mindful that these generalities pertain largely to males and that female addicts "appear to have a wider variety of sources of income other than property crime by which to support a drug habit" (Brownfield 1996, 133).

3. Although Miller was concerned, at least in part, with the process by which lower-class culture generates gang delinquency, his primary concern was with the distinctive class-based culture that dominates lower-class lifestyles, ideologies, and behaviors. As a result, he determined that certain behavior develops from social interaction among poor individuals (especially men) as they are socialized on relying, not on wealth and widely accepted notions of social status, but on street savvy, toughness, and other characteristics.

4. David Matza and Gresham Sykes (1961) earlier pointed to "subterranean traditions" within the conventional culture that are important to deviant subcultures because they are tolerated, within limits, by legitimate society. Thus, criminals (both street and white-collar) are seen as conforming to subterranean cultural traditions when easy money becomes a valued objective. In fact, wealth motivations, monetary success, greed, and consumption are all positive qualities in American society and are specific to crime (both street and suite).

4

CONSCIOUSNESS AND PROPERTY CRIME

A central theoretical and empirical issue to the class-crime link (and especially crimes committed by underclass, chronic, property offenders) is explaining class-based consciousness and its relevance to actors' behavior.[1] There are differing interpretations of and opinions on this issue. One opinion is that property crime is a manifestation of embryonic class-consciousness. In this interpretation, property criminals are defined as economically deprived, potential rebels against private property, its ownership, and wealth inequalities. Another interpretation is that property crime is little more than subculturally sanctioned illicit behavior whose participants have little recognition of or commitment to class interests. In this interpretation, property offenders' behavior is evidenced by their hedonistic lifestyles and irrational and spontaneous actions. Because of these two diverse views on this issue, persistent criminals are treated theoretically as both antisystemic class players (e.g., among some Left idealism) and hedonistic individualists with no antisystemic consciousness (e.g., among the Right and some Left realism). The reality, from evidence to date, may actually embody a bit of both explanations.

Explaining consciousness among persistent offenders has been either neglected or politicized. Left idealism, for example, at times has treated property criminals as both victims of expropriative economic relations and rebels against such as indicated in their criminal enterprises. Left realism has, occasionally, treated property criminals as working-class members preying on others like them. In this context, they are unaware of the political and economic dimensions of their crimes.

Continual reliance on the idealist-realist dichotomy for understanding street crime—as action and our continuing use of particular forms of class-based language and terminology has left the politics of repetitive crime an unexplored and sometimes ambiguously dismissed phenomenon. To date, sociologies of crime largely ignore the likelihood that street crime, and especially crimes committed by those who live off it, "contains elements of an unmentioned and perhaps unconscious political protest" against economic inequalities, political injustice and the absence of decent jobs (Gans 1995, 80).

Most politically motivated actors, whether functioning solely to benefit themselves or a collective, possess some degree of awareness or consciousness of their plight, their ultimate aspirations, the strictures on their lives, and the strategies for linking their objectives to action. In other words, they exhibit a consciousness about their reality and goals and commit themselves to strategies that reconcile the disjuncture between them. Unlike consciousness that is manifest in more sophisticated political action, however, criminal consciousness may materialize in simple garden-variety street crimes, with little recognition of or articulation by the actors themselves of political aspirations and strategies.

Earlier observations are that street crime is connected implicitly and explicitly to economic and political inequalities. Although perhaps acting with little direct consciousness regarding such, there remains the assumption that "there is no criminal so stupid but recognizes this terrible fact, though he may not be able to account for it" (Goldman 1969, 116). Property criminals indeed may be engaged in political action of sorts, but it is unlike that exhibited by reflective, articulate, and methodically strategic political actors (e.g., corporate and political criminals). Property criminals may not be able to recognize the politics of their actions; their attention may be fully committed to the immediacy of their wants and needs at the foreground of their actions while in the throes of poverty, drug addictions, poor job prospects, and an absence of social capital. Although largely unrecognized by the actors themselves, consciousness among persistent offenders may simply represent a different manifestation of politicized action from that more commonly found within class-based market societies.

Traditional explanations of class-conscious actors (and especially workers) are not particularly helpful for accounting for repetitive property crimes. Neither do they apply to most white-collar crimes, both of which are committed by individuals and organized groups with little recognition of class strategies and political agenda. Traditional interpretations of class-consciousness and praxis are applied to certain political crimes and criminals—when the politicized crimes represent class or status group interests, peoples' struggles, and liberation movements. Yet, most political crime is committed for political advantage rather than class objectives. Consciousness, in this case, is centered on attaining political rather than class goals. At times, both political and class agendas converge, but the driving force among political crime is to effect or prevent largely political rather than economic change. Thus, political crimes, such as terrorism, which often includes both property and violent illegalities, implicitly contains a shared meaning that is not common among property or violent crimes and criminals (see e.g., Ross 2002). Yet, the central distinction between property and violent crimes and terrorism is mainly explained by offenders' political motivation or ideology. For the most part, terrorists have "well developed ideologies and codes of behavior" that do not exist among property and violent street criminals. Unlike most street and white-collar crimes, "ideology provides the motivating force behind terrorism" and helps shape "acceptable methods for achieving their goals" (Lynch and Groves 1989, 39).

Few property and violent criminals demonstrate sophisticated or well thought out ideologies that are a part of terrorism. Thus, class-consciousness, as an explanation for behavior, mostly would not apply to white-collar or political crimes and criminals. The actions of lower-class property offenders who operate within distinct criminal subcultures may express consciousness of other, less obvious dimensions than those of terrorists or unified workers.

Class-consciousness, much like class itself, has not been well formulated in the literature and is grounds for much debate among, for example, structural- and humanist-Marxism. One central controversy in the class-consciousness debate has been over issues of whether individuals write their own history—meaning—are they "authors of their own acts." Related questions have nearly always been raised about "whether intentions have explanatory power [and] whether the distinction between 'subjects' and 'objects' is an admissible one" (E. Wright 1985, 241). This argument, in other words, centers on long-standing differences over another dichotomy within sociology—the significance of structure versus agency.

Recent research on class location and adjudication has examined the *consciousness* concept. Consciousness is treated as a subjective condition and *"accessible to the individual's own awareness.* Consciousness is thus counterpoised to unconsciousness" (E. Wright 1985, 244; see also Wright 1997). Class-consciousness has received considerable attention in Marxian and neo-Marxian amalgamations. Two specific interpretations dominate these traditions. The first, a Hegelian/Lukacs explication, focuses on individual occupants of a class location and how they "would feel and believe if they were rational" actors. The second emphasizes the importance of collectively shared ideologies and actions that emerge within "supra-individual entities" (E. Wright 1985, 242 and 243). From these interpretations, consciousness is thus attached to both class as aggregate and to the individuals who occupy them, their choices, and their actions. No matter the interpretation, the literature does not suggest a simple, deterministic interpretation that "class actors are automatons, unconsciously playing out scripts in a drama." Rather, the broadest explanation includes structure and agency. "Class action is much more heavily determined by the concrete choices and pressures that people face in given circumstances than by any stable or enduring patterns of consciousness" (E. Wright 1985, 144). There remains the theoretical position, supported by historical events, that class unity, consciousness, and struggle emerge in change-oriented structural and potentially revolutionary group behavior.

Most theories of class-based struggle, peoples' movements, and revolution have focused heavily on participants. Most accounts are reducible to social-psychological explanations by emphasizing the social actors' perceptions, frustrations, motivations, and allegiances. These arguments fall short of social-structural and comparative-historical explanations that are highly relevant to the few cases of class-conscious mass behavior and revolutions in modern world history.

Some explanations of these movements have focused on relative deprivation as an indicator of class location, immiseration, and eventual class action. However, Theda Skocpol (1976), among others, is critical of the concept and its place in accounting for revolutionary development. The criticism is that relative deprivation, defined as "a perceived discrepancy," is similar to a frustration-aggression indicator that ultimately is reducible to a psychological rather than a historical-materialist explanation. The latter takes into account social developments, such as internal contradictions and the loss of the legitimacy of dominant order. Relative deprivation, when related to participation in political violence or antisystemic behavior, has proven insignificant; in some cases, it is the least consequential variable for predicting political activism for economic change. Some have characterized Marxist explanations of revolutions, which locate their causes and consequences in socioeconomic developments, as exemplary. Others suggest, "Marxist-derived theories of revolutionary processes cannot be uncritically accepted as rigorous, empirically validated explanations." Even by pedestrian observation, we must admit that modern day revolutions are far more complex and simply "cannot be comprehended in strictly class terms" (Skocpol 1976, 172–73).

There are other problems with relative deprivation when explaining consciousness-inspired group action. Relative deprivation, by nominal and operational definition, implies a consciousness that theoretically forms into group or class-level awareness that its situation, relative to others, is worse.

Left unexplained are the mechanisms and processes by which such comparative knowledge is produced. Also unexplained is the amount of socioeconomic difference at levels necessary and sufficient to account for an individual's, let alone a group's realization that things are differentially distributed. Unlike relative deprivation as explanation, poverty does not implicitly require individual or group awareness that things are unfair relative to others. Poverty is an existence rather than a comparative position to more affluent individuals. But, relative deprivation remains an important concept, especially when applied to individual criminal rather than collective action, and it is given attention elsewhere in this book (see chapters 3 and 6). After all, poverty in the midst of plenty can be a powerful and important force for setting actions into motion.

Based on recent comparative observation, class consciousness has been dissected into several key elements. Each is pertinent to the issues of consciousness and actions among repetitive property offenders. The first element is one's perceptions of alternative behaviors or courses of action or "the subjective perception of what possibilities exist." Class consciousness, in this regard, "involves the ways in which the perceptions of alternatives have a class content" (E. Wright 1985, 247). Deciding for crime implicitly contains a selection for that course of action from among a set of perceived alternative courses of action. Perceptions of alternative behaviors may or may not reflect the real material alternatives available, but perceptions determine just what available courses of action offenders believe exist. Various studies with chronic street criminals confirm that offenders recognize few alternatives to continued criminal behavior due to class location, subcultural socialization, and consciousness.

Second is one's perceived consequences of action or the range of alternative actions. This component implies theoretical thinking among actors as they attempt to predict outcomes from choices. This means that people must have some appreciation, theoretically at least, for anticipated consequences of a given choice of action. In other words, choice about innumerable matters in life involves theory. "Class consciousness, in these terms, revolves around the ways in which the theories people hold shape the choices they make around class practices" (E. Wright 1985, 247). People's ability to link action to consequence remains an ongoing concern for research and theoretical development. This remains especially difficult with research on repetitive property offenders and their choices, material conditions, subcultures, and lifestyles. Pertinent to this element of consciousness is perception and its relevance to one's social class. Chronic offenders, as is argued here, share class location but display little awareness of their mutual class interests and less about strategies for linking conscious action to class or subcultural prosperity.

Preference for choosing one action over another is the third component of class-consciousness. Class-consciousness has to do with the subjective specification of class interests (E. Wright 1985, 247). In other words, consciousness should reflect individuals' assessment of the desirability of actions and consequences. Selecting a course of action undoubtedly is determined, in part, by preference. This is relevant to repetitive property offenders who, as a group, realize that few options exist for them to maintain their desired lifestyle. In many cases, persistent crime may be that preferred course of action, especially given offenders' commitment to street culture, easy money, expensive drugs, fashion, and maintaining autonomous lifestyles. Yet, among property offenders, class preferences may have little to do with their crimes; they may have even less to do with their crimes as a sort of politics-in-action.

Chronic street offenders share many similarities. A small part of the underclass, repetitive offenders share some commonalities with their fellow class members. The underclass (and street criminals within it) theoretically, at least, possesses some degree of class-based revolutionary power. It historically has remained unaware of it or, at least, impotent at using it. Its political consciousness has fluctuated and has been unstable as it has manifested itself in such divergent activities as rioting against state authority on one hand and participating in antilabor strikes on the other.[2]

Underclass members "typically have not thought or acted in revolutionary ways at all. Even as they have fueled the greatest social revolutions, [they] have fought for traditional and either specific or parochial values and goals" (Skocpol 1976, 164). For the most part, underclass members historically have remained oblivious to the potential threat that they may pose to social order, if by nothing more than their growing numbers within market societies. Its class members are unconscious. Their unconsciousness is perhaps best explained by their relationships to and experiences with production-consumption processes. Displaced from regularly functioning as wage laborers, the poor are not subjected to ongoing expropriative exploitation. Without that relationship, they are not exposed to conditions that theoretically give rise to class consciousness. Within theoretical explications, work is and remains a precursor to alienation and class struggle, without which few antecedent conditions for the development of class-based consciousness exist. Workers engage in the activity that they commonly share—work—characterized by social relationships dependent on the expropriation of surplus value (E. Wright 1985, 184). Workers, unlike street criminals, participate in legitimate, labor-related struggles over scarce resources. Therefore, they, hypothetically, have more reason than burglars, for example, to recognize and articulate their common plight as class-based. However, workers also rarely explain their material conditions in such terms.

Although independent of each other, those who live off crime participate in similar income-generating activities (e.g., burglary and robbery). To some extent, theirs is an occupation with commonly shared social antecedents, motivations, and objectives. Their work, as much as anything, represents their common bond. They, after all, are marginal players in an individualist, market-driven culture and, to some extent, compete among themselves over scarce resources (as do members of other classes) yet outside of officially sanctioned, expropriative labor processes. However, they do not overtly define their commonly shared situations as resulting from their collective experiences, cultures, and, most important, social class.

Street criminals' work, committed largely by poor people, is highly individualistic, hedonistic, and generally "not connected to any broad conception of social and political change" (E. Wright 1973, 16). Although crime contains potentially rebellious behavior by displaced and dehumanized individuals, it generally is somewhat controlled, and offenders, to some extent, are contained by the criminal justice system. There remains little indication, despite early, Left idealist criminology stating otherwise, that crime among persistent property offenders is class-motivated rebellion or at any level indicative of group consciousness. In other words, although "street crime might arise out of social, political and economic conditions, it is not a progressive political expression." It is unlikely to contribute to structural or long-term solutions to social problems and, in fact, may be dysfunctional to peoples' movements as "it divides the working class, nourishes racism, popularizes law and order campaigns, victimizes the poor, consolidates the threat of violence towards women and increases the vulnerability of poor neighborhoods" (Scraton and Chadwick 1991, 172). Criminals' behavior largely is opportunistic and mostly unsophisticated with evidence of little or no class appreciation.

In the final analysis, we are left with the realization that chronic offenders' stated rationale for their behavior lacks any class-based political motive. Perhaps other unstated motivations are at work. Or, perhaps, rather than class and class consciousness, their actions result from their independence from each other and official culture and as manifestations of their subcultures.

PROPERTY CRIME AS RESISTANCE

Repetitive property offenders, who, in the main, are underclass members, undoubtedly have little understanding of and appreciation for class analyses, structures, consciousness, and action. Yet, there is something about their consciousness and behavior that is, to some extent, antisystemic (although they may not always realize it and mostly fail to articulate it). They may understand their actions but "may not have at [their] disposal a language or a discourse which can make real sense of [their] actions to others and privilege them with real historical understandings" (Presdee 2000, 22). Their crimes, from time to time and ongoing for some, represent a resistance of sorts to material and symbolic manifestations of authority.

At other times, their crimes are committed for the sheer pleasure derived from simply carrying out the act itself. Crime has a particular meaning for them that alone may be enough to continue choosing for and engaging in it. At other times, offenders' behavior can be characterized as retreatist. A subtle way of resisting, retreatism is a withdrawal from participating in officially approved activities of work and leisure. For example, those committed to street crime as a way of life refuse to work and dislike others who do; they don't vote; they reject formal education; they have little use for and investment in the conducts and credentials that allow for participation in legitimate society (e.g., developing a work record, acquiring job skills, curbing their alcohol and drug use, withdrawing from street culture); they participate in drug and street culture; and they often maintain nomadic lifestyles. These attitudes, ideologies, and lifestyles may represent a style of resistance and independence—a form of hedonistic anarchism, or what has elsewhere been termed, "experiential anarchism" (Lyng 1990).

Their retreating may well be, among other behaviors, an act of resistance to authority or simply to mainstream culture and its widely accepted attributes. After all, mainstream culture and the values reflected therein, are not very appealing to street-centered burglars, robbers, and thieves. Mainstream culture values traits such as hard work, delayed gratification, sobriety, a family, a home, and job stability. These men's lived behaviors are contralegitimacy. They are not only deviant, they are also oppositional.

Retreating may also be an act of defiance. Individuals, both criminal and noncriminal, often choose to retreat in various ways, and their behaviors often indicate personal displays of resistance and defiance. For example, some individuals, regardless of their class, choose not to watch television. Others choose not to vote. Refusing to participate in television viewing and voting symbolize a resistance to dominant cultural forces generated externally to individuals. It is a passive resistance. Some who choose to "throw away their TV," as the song goes, or to stay home on election day, oftentimes exhibit a certain confidence about their decisions to withdraw. They display a morality of the high ground, so to speak, believing that television is composed of lousy programming and voting a meaningless choice between parallel candidates, parties, and platforms. Those who continue participating in such activities, so goes the logic, have failed to realize their futility.

There is something political at work in these behaviors. Retreating from television viewing, like voting, is a moral, ideological, and political decision based on the belief that each is a vain exercise. In other words, retreatists in these cases display a different degree of consciousness about dominant culture and the seemingly meaningless choices presented to them in the forms of politics and smart programming. Retreatists believe that those who continue viewing and voting remain uncritical and unconscious of the hoodwinking forces at work, or are happy enough to continue participating in them. When one's decision to no longer vote or watch television is made known, others typically show surprise or disbelief, since the popular belief is that television viewing keeps one attuned to popular culture while voting keeps one involved in a transparent democracy. Apparently, a different realization or consciousness of sorts is at work among those who retreat.

Career street criminals likewise may be engaging in a conscious yet passive resistance by refusing to work or to engage in other "world-taken-for-granted" activities (Berger 1963, 117). Their commitment to street life, drug culture, and free-spiritedness symbolizes political resistance. Yet, their political-economic consciousness is unsophisticated, especially when compared to class-conscious resistance in the traditional interpretation. This does not imply that there is nothing political, symbolic, or defiant at work among persistent street offenders. Like nonvoters and nonviewers, street criminals disassociate themselves from legitimacy by not working or voting. They believe that the straight world holds little for them. After all, they have seen through the vain exercise of working for a wage, especially given their limitations to do just that.

Retreatist behavior and lifestyle, for some, are manifestations of resistance to authority. Chronic offenders who have serious drug addictions, more so than those without drug problems, tend to live in isolation from others. Both criminal and drug-abusing behaviors are withdrawals from society and its behavioral expectations. Yet, in each case, the resistance is a quiet one. Rather than an abstract, politicized ideology, resistance of this sort among repeat offenders allows them privacy to go about their lives by regularly participating in, yet with little thought given to, oppositional behavior (see Tunnell 2004, chap. 5).

Rather than simply dismiss street crime as absent political meaning, which some criminology suggests, we might better account for deviance by understanding "the situated politics of crime and criminality [and recognize that] . . . acts of crime . . . must also carry some degree of political meaning" (Ferrell 1997, 151). In this way, chronic offenders may well be rebels, but without a cause. Their rebellion is against everything and nothing. They rebel against inequalities in wealth and capital, yet they prey on the poor and working classes; they are opposed to mainstream values, yet they commit crimes as a means of participating in consumption processes; their very actions suggest that they oppose state authority, yet they accept state definitions of crime. They define their situations as an "us against them" conflict, yet, rather than unified, they remain disparate and disconnected. They may embody something very real in anarchism. They are walking, talking, and acting contradictions, constructing their own realities and resistances of and against social life. Yet, they have no master plan, no political agenda, and no long-term objectives. Rather, they make things up as they go along. They opportunistically and spontaneously commit crimes all while remaining true to some semblance of resistance to authority, however they may define it. Mark Hamm (1993) once referred to skinheads as "idiots with ideology." Compared to skinheads' highly developed and propagated political-race strategies, persistent property offenders possess (or at least display) little ideology. Repetitive property offenders do engage in rebellious behavior, but they are mostly absent, well-informed, and mutually shared ideologies found among politically or racially motivated offenders; they engage in their crimes primarily as political or lifestyle struggles (Weber 1946). Chronic street criminals perhaps should be considered rebels without a *stated* cause.

Contemporary criminals are vastly different from those of only a few generations ago, evidenced, to some degree, by the absence of a criminal code and the near absence of trust among them (Austin and Irwin 2001). In other words, there is little collective ideology and behavior. A major sentiment among them is "'You have to look out for number one.' . . . Street life, with its emphasis on enjoyment of the moment, discourages the formation of close, long-lasting ties" (Wright and Decker 1994, 76). This recent development within criminal subcultures suggests that little cohesion or substantive intimacy exists among their members. They do not view their interests as fundamental to their occupation, race, or social class. As a result, there is little if any collective consciousness and even fewer activities that can be remotely characterized as class or group-based. Rather, offenders are disparate, disconnected, politically immature individualists who display few behaviors for the good of their cohort. Yet, as individuals, they are involved in their own forms of disruptive actions that they realize are contrary to socially approved behaviors (with the exception, of course, that they are hedonistic, materially motivated behaviors, which are fundamental to those engaged in both legitimate and illegitimate enterprises within market societies).

Although they are very much a part of groups with their own subcultural exigencies, they continually display behaviors that are valued within dominant culture. For example, Dannie "Red Hog" Martin describes prisoners' reflections on the Persian Gulf War and their participation in the prison's industrial complex running assembly lines at double time. One convict, according to Martin, claimed that

> I want us to win, but I also hope it drags on for a while. They are spending a lot of money on this war, and I'm hoping they will have to use some of that money they've put aside to build prisons with (Martin and Sussman 1993, 277).

Martin's observations show that at least some prisoners are concerned with the prison building binge and the near exponential growth in captives to the point that they support warfare abroad to warfare at home against others like them—the poor, young, and largely nonwhite.

Crime as resistance most likely is *not* a manifestation of class-based consciousness in action. The resistance itself presumably originates in a variety of places and develops largely through subculturally based ideology. This phenomenon may have as great an impact on crime-as-resistance as social class does on class-based defiance. The resistance may be personal, individual, and defiant. It may be subculturally or situationally bounded. The relevant issue is that it includes activities that are apart from the Official World, its strictures, and its cultural controls (Denton 1990).

Such activities and their locations demand that sociology ask the right kinds of questions. For example, "the question thus becomes, not 'Is this crime or resistance?' but 'In what ways might the participants in this event be conscious of, and resistant to, the contradictions in which they are caught?'" (Ferrell 1992, 120). It is this recognition of resistance that demands that we not simply dismiss criminals' actions as apolitical. It also suggests that, at the same time, we not romanticize their lifestyles, cultures, or defiance. Thus, in this case, neither Left idealism nor Left realism adequately explains their actions.

Property offenders' resistance to authority is demonstrated by their abhorrence of legitimate work. It is also obvious in their disdain for formal education. Consider, for example, the following conversation with an incarcerated armed robber:

> Q. You say you hated school? Why did you?
> A. I think it was authority more or less. In fact, to this day, I've got a worse hate for school than I do the penitentiary system (Tunnell 1992, 121).

Akerstrom's (1985, 83) subjects were dismayed with law-abiders' inability to see the system as they characterized it, and especially education and work, as unfair, demanding, and offering few rewards. For example:

> I just can't see why ordinary people don't see through the system. They'll work their ass off and they'll die before retiring.

And another's comments on "ordinary people":

> I don't dislike them, but I feel sorry for them. They live all their lives toiling and wearing themselves out, complaining about their jobs and their bosses and they never get any money.

Furthermore, several of Wright and Decker's (1997, 46) active armed robbers, like the subjects of other studies, rejected work altogether. For example:

> I just don't believe in work. There is enough shit on this earth right here for everybody, nobody should have to be suffering. You shouldn't have to suffer and work like no dog for it, I'm just a firm believer in that. I'll go out there and try to take what I believe I got coming because ain't nobody gonna walk up and give it to me. I commit stickups because I'm broke and need money; it's just what I'm gonna do. I'm not going to work! That's out! I'm through with work. I done had twenty-five or thirty jobs in my little lifetime and that's out. I can't do it! I'm not going to!

Other criminals' descriptions of borrowing money for a temporary solution indicate that they often choose crime as defiant action over the legitimate act of groveling for money.

> It's there for the taking but it ain't there for the loaning (Tunnell 1992, 65).

Street offenders clearly recognize income inequalities that, at some level, play a part in predatory behavior. The following conversation is illustrative:

A. Let me tell you, a lot of people make me madder than hell.

Q. What kind of people?

A. Well people that ain't got shit can't get nothing from the people that has got it. I still get real pissed about that.

Q. Do you mean about how unfair things are?

A. Yeah. Like they advertise about those kids, the one's overseas. They're always on the radio asking for money, you know, send twenty dollars to adopt a kid, you know, and all this shit. The sons-of-bitches around here has got thousands of dollars laying up in a bank getting rusty and they won't send them kids a damn dime (Tunnell 1990, 52).

Persistent property offenders also display their resistance to authority and culturally approved behavior by actively and openly celebrating criminal acts. They take pleasure in committing crime. Just as with skydiving, risky skateboarding, high-speed motorcycle riding, and bridge jumping, the momentary excitement and thrill are as important as the accomplishment. The process of successfully engaging in edgework and in "getting over" straights, squares, and cultural controls, unlike activities approved by official society, offer sheer pleasure, an adrenaline rush, and excitement. The excitement is a momentary break from an otherwise monotonous lifestyle. Excitement is again indicative of a focal concern, as described in chapter 3.

The following conversation indicates the thrill of risky behavior. In this case, though, the actor increases the excitement level by intentionally elevating the risk component.

Q. So, how often would you shoplift?

A. Anytime I could. Anytime that I only stood a 50 percent chance of making it. Sometimes if I only stood a 25 percent chance of doing it, I would do it, because I enjoyed it. I'm the type of person, man, if I could steal something from way in the back row or if the store manager is standing here and I could take something right under his nose, that's what I'd get.

Q. Why would you prefer that?

A. Because it's more of an accomplishment. There wasn't anything that I enjoyed more than shoplifting (Tunnell 1992, 122–24).

Another accomplished burglar who went on stealing binges describes the excitement of and meaning assigned to his crimes:

A. It got to be a game. I've been locked up since I was sixteen. I've wasted the best years of my life. I can never get them back because I've played this game of "I'm going to beat them." And then you get to that stage, you wonder, "Who in the hell is it I'm trying to beat?" It's just like a chess game. I'm trying to stay a step ahead. I mean, fuck, it's a challenge. I mean, by God, it gets down to where it's just me against them and that's the way it is. To me getting over on him or beating him at this game is 90 percent of it. The fucking money ain't nothing. Getting over on them is what it is. It got to be where I just liked it.

Q. What did you like about it?

A. The excitement and the feeling of, you know, I fucked them, I mean I had got over on them. They put their best investigators on me and I fucked them. . . . Crime was a game with a whole lot of reality (Tunnell 1992, 46).

This is defiant resistance. The resistance, in part, reflects a subculturally engendered consciousness as offenders of a particular social class, committed to living off crime, internalize and openly display focal concerns of autonomy and excitement. These traits become the salient life themes of persistent offenders who, as they become further entrenched in subcultural and personal resistance, increasingly withdraw from dominant culture and whatever it values. The resistance is qualitatively different from, say, a Timothy McVeigh, whose actions revealed his consciousness and ideology (Hamm 1997). Unlike politically motivated actors, street criminals' inaction, withdrawal, and culture avoidance are manifestations of their consciousness and defiant resistance. Street crime, and especially crime as a way of life, becomes a contra existence, an adventure in a parallel universe where norms, values, and actions are oftentimes opposite those central to dominant culture. For chronic property offenders, class, culture, and focal concerns coalesce and give meaning to actions and shared ways of life.

Rather than class struggle per se, property offenders' consciousness is manifest in crimes themselves—their edgework. This is especially the case with repeat offenders, given their social class, the socioeconomic conditions within which they live, and the broader context within which their actions take place. Their crimes may be the "direct antithesis of role behavior in the institutional domain" as the skills that they value and that are central to their edgework—spontaneity, impulsivity, and posturing—are used to control others as well as unpredictable and dangerous situations (Lyng 1990, 864).

This edgework, or experiential anarchy, is spontaneous or creative action and is contrary to constrained, institutional expectations. Restriction as opposed to free-spirited, nomadic spontaneity may be especially apropos to those most constrained by hierarchical strictures—the dispossessed and the successfully labeled. Crime-as-action may represent an important counter-activity for street offenders in their daily activities and lived realities, more so than for others who are less constrained by class and labeling.

Explicating edgework as a form of conscious experiential anarchism, Stephen Lyng (1990, 869), drawing from Marx and Mead, suggests that individuals, denied the possibility of realizing their species nature—that unique human experience—whether in material production or social relationships, drift through life with an underdeveloped sense of self. The dispossessed, drug-addicted, and labeled convicts experience little rewarding in the way of material or social relations. As a result, their experiences likely develop into a narcissistic lifestyle leading them in various directions, including crime, as a response to their material and social scarcities. Crime offers them opportunities to use skills that are devalued in production processes and that, in the main, are "purged from the labor process" (Lyng 1990, 871).

Crime, as edgework, is a "desired choice—a way of fulfilling unmet needs . . . involv[ing] the use of specific skills" (Lyng 1990, 871). Skills alone that are central to edgework are devalued in legitimate material productions yet are linked with abilities to "maintain control of a situation that verges on total chaos. It is this ability that edgeworkers believe most determines success or failure in negotiating the edge, and the chance to exercise this 'survival skill' seems to be what they value most" (Lyng 1990, 871). To survive, edgeworkers must negotiate unexpected dangers. "But the ultimate challenge is to survive those hazards that cannot be anticipated, that require the use of one's innate survival ability" (Lyng 1990, 875). Thus, edgeworkers involved in experiential anarchy rely on gut-level instincts, survival skills, flexibility, innovation, and spontaneous action, each of which distinguishes their labor from those working within legitimate production and consumption processes and cultures. Their consciousness is one that embraces and reflects a contrary way of life. As one repeat offender living at the edge told me, "I've always done what I wanted to do. Damn the consequences" (Private interview 1987).

Understanding consciousness means developing a rich appreciation of the foreground of crime, the immediacy of action, the meanings assigned to behaviors, and the many forms that consciousness may take. Consciousness may also be revealed in everyday activities as actors create their social worlds and their own good reasons for thinking and acting (or acting without thinking) about class, poverty, inequalities, or resistance. If postmodernism has raised our consciousness about any single event, it is that reality is constructed in human activities as diverse as burglary, skydiving, teaching, and writing.

NOTES

1. *Behavior* seemingly is a more appropriate concept than *action*, since behavior includes action and inaction, each of which logically is associated with both objective and subjective conceptualizations of social class and consciousness.

2. This fickle characteristic has been well documented by Marx's (1934) analysis of the French Revolution, Mark Traugott's (1985) description of the Parisian Insurrection, and Skocpol's (1979) theoretical treatment of revolution.

5

VICTIMS AND VICTIMIZATION

Crime in America is hardly uniformly distributed or randomly occurring. Crime and victimization are unevenly dispersed across groups, time, and space. For example, violent crime within America's inner cities most often involves people of color as both victim and victimizer. Young, black, urban males are victims of violent crimes at far greater rates than any other group. In rural America, white males are typically the perpetrators of violent and property crimes (see, e.g., Weisheit et al. 1999, chap. 1).

Data also indicate that certain crimes vary by time of year. Violent crime tends to increase during the hot summer months. Some recent research shows that commercial robberies peak during winter months, presumably because winter clothing offers opportunities for disguises and businesses enjoy greater cash flows with increased year-end shopping (e.g., Jansen and Van Koppen 1999). Time of day and the day of the week are also associated with variance in crime rates.

Crime and victimization are not consistent across history as crime has increased and decreased during the decades of recordkeeping with lower rates in the early part of the twenty-first century than in the mid-1980s. Gender and age are closely related to crime and victimization as young people are both offenders and victims at rates far higher than the elderly. Women, more than men, are victims of sexual assault, violence, and harassment (and especially in the home) (e.g., DeKeseredy et al. 2003).

Data on the distribution of property crime consistently show that victims mostly are poor and working-class people and small businesses, while those least often touched are middle and affluent classes and large corporations. Property crime victimization rates are highest for families earning between $7,500 and $10,000 annually; for residential burglary, rates are highest among low-income tenants and specifically nonwhites that earn less than

$7,500 annually (Laub 1997; Miethe and McCorkle 1998, 128). This skewing of victimization by victims' social class is mostly attributed to the convergence of offenders, potential targets, and criminogenic places and situations.

Those street criminals who are of particular concern to this work—highly active, repetitive, adult property offenders—while seeking criminal opportunities or targets, rarely venture far from their homes or neighborhoods. Repetitive property criminals operate within spaces that they know reasonably well, while preying daily on those living around them and their property. In other words, offenders select targets within their "awareness space," that is, neighborhoods within which they are familiar and within which they can find suitable victims (Bursik and Grasmick 1993, chap. 3). As a result, they discover easily available prey among people like themselves—poor and working-class individuals within the immediate vicinity.

The confinements of space are significant for understanding the intraclass and race complexities of property crime and victimization. Crime in reality is local, unevenly distributed, and affecting certain categories of people more than others (Ruggiero 1992, 127). Victimization is far from simply the "product, or end result, of a particular set of social or other determinants" (Lea 1992, 83). Entirely random victimization, whether a violent or property crime, is not typical given what we know about the web of relationships and the importance of locality. In poor parts of some inner cities in the United States and Canada, victims often know those who prey upon them, although the majority of robbery victims report that their assailants are strangers (DeKeseredy et al. 2003; Karmen 1996).

From the research to date, social class has been conclusively and consistently connected to victimization at both the individual and aggregate levels. Research shows that high concentrations of poor families within a community experience elevated rates of violent and property crime while higher socioeconomic communities experience lower rates (Hagan 1994, 88).

Theoretical and empirical works among both the ideological and political Left and Right have long described, unlike early national surveys, the uneven distribution of crime in the United States. As a result, left realism, among other contemporary schools, for example, has relied on and propagated the use of local crime surveys to more accurately measure crime among oft-neglected yet most often victimized populations (e.g., Walklate 1992).

Data on victims (and especially data from national or centralized sources) are widely recognized as offering incomplete accounts, due in part to victims' reluctance to report certain crimes and the recording processes used by legal authorities. For example, research indicates that police are more likely to record crimes in more affluent neighborhoods than in poor ones. Poor victims are often left out of the official count. In fact, the single most important variable that explains police officers' nonrecording of residential burglary is the victims' impoverished status.

Recent research supports the underclass or benign neglect hypothesis which suggests that communities with high concentrations of poor people and people of color "receive less public service, including police service, than white middle-class neighborhoods, largely because these neighborhoods and their residents are undervalued" (Warner 1997, 633). Other than simply benign neglect as explanation for marginalizing the poor's victimization, a second assumption is that police consider such neighborhoods criminogenic. Composed of poor, unemployed, nonwhite individuals who likely may have experienced multigenerational poverty, police may consider residents of these crime-filled communities as less deserving of their services than those of more affluent neighborhoods (Warner 1997). Since police repeatedly respond to all sorts of crime problems in poor neighborhoods, they may come to define nearly all residents and activities as suspicious, deviant, or criminal. Police practices of this sort further marginalize the social problem of victimization.

Poor victims, like poor offenders, are living in increasingly marginalized spaces and may be "heading toward a dystopia of exclusion" (Young 1999; DeKeseredy et al. 2003, 25). Such an interpretation also emphasizes poor victims' inability to reduce their victimization through formal police operations and informal social controls within their own neighborhoods. The neighborhoods themselves are generally considered socially disorganized, which means that particular neighborhood characteristics shape neighbors' inabilities to monitor and control social deviance and criminal activities.

Social disorganization, as a social-ecology explanation for crime variation across space, has roots in the Chicago School and particularly in the work of Robert Parks, Ernest Burgess, and Roderick McKenzie (1925) and Clifford Shaw and Henry McKay (1942). Contemporary social science continues to use social disorganization as an organizing motif (see, e.g., Rose and Clear 1998). The major issue for this school of thought is accounting for consistently high rates of crime and victimization in specific places or neighborhoods. Neighborhoods considered socially disorganized have particular characteristics. In the main, those communities are ethnically heterogeneous and are populated by residents of low socioeconomic status. The neighborhoods experience high levels of residential mobility and family disruption. These characteristics result in a community's social disorganization that manifests itself in residents with few friendship networks, low levels of organizational participation, and little supervision of young people (Sampson and Groves 1989, 783). Residents of these communities do not get to know their neighbors, do not monitor their neighbors' children, and do not participate in organizations of, for example, parent-teacher associations, youth groups, boy scouts, and others that are valued in middle-class communities with residential stability.

The concept, *collective efficacy* is generally used along with social disorganization to describe residents' trust of one another and their ability and willingness to "intervene on behalf of the common good, specifically to supervise children and maintain public order" (Sampson, Raudenbush, and Earls 1998, 1). In neighborhoods with high levels of collective efficacy, residents' relationships are intimate. There, residents count on one another for social support, such as watching out for their children or intervening if adolescents engage in deviant behaviors. Neighborhoods that are socially disorganized have low levels of collective efficacy. Inner-city neighborhoods, for example, with low levels of collective efficacy, are those most likely to experience higher levels of property and violent crimes and victimization (e.g., DeKeseredy et al. 2003).

The recently integrated "multicontextual criminal opportunity theory" links environmental factors of community, for example, to individual offender characteristics to account for crime and victimization patterns. Connecting a routine activities approach to social control approaches, this theory focuses on "the conditions necessary for an *act* of crime or victimization—a criminal event—to occur" (Wilcox, Land, and Hunt 2003, 45). This theory treats disorganized neighborhoods as "bounded locales" that foster dense populations of motivated offenders and potentially vulnerable victims. Absent capable guardianship over person or property, and given such neighborhoods' lack of collective efficacy, victims are defined as suitable targets by the disproportionate number of would-be predators within those social spaces (Wilcox et al. 2003, chap. 3).

Similar to the skewed victimization from street crime, the poor and working class, more often than the nonpoor, are direct victims of corporate and state-corporate transgressions. Activities such as situating a toxic waste dump, an incinerator, a landfill, or a highway extension near poor or working-class neighborhoods are common. Workers placed in harm's way by corporate decisions, by definition, are there because of hierarchy. Typical victims of crime, whether garden-variety street crimes or corporate transgressions, remain out of sight of most people and, as a result, out of the public mind.

Other variables, some of which are connected to social class, also are related to street crime victimization risks. For example, one assessment of recent research shows that "both offenders and victims tend to be in the same groups: young, male, and unmarried" (Felson 1994, 21). Furthermore, self-report surveys and official data indicate that "not only are rates of offending and arrest high in African American communities, but so too are rates of victimization. That is, crime is predominantly intraracial" (Hagan and Peterson 1995, 23). Recent data from a National Crime Victimization Survey also indicate that those who are at greatest risk of victimization from that most serious property crime—robbery—are

> men rather than women, minorities rather than members of the white majority, young persons more than middle-age or elderly people, single or divorced individuals over married couples, poor people rather than those who are better off financially . . . less-educated persons more than those with better educations, and city residents rather than people living in suburbs or small towns. Combining these factors, the profile of the person facing the highest risks of all is that of a poor, African-American young man living in an inner-city neighborhood who dropped out of high school. . . . The highest robbery rate . . . was for black teenagers between the ages of sixteen and nineteen (Karmen 1995, 81–82; cf., Miethe and McCorkle 1998, chap. 4).

From the research to date, we learn of such economic-crime and victim relationships from aggregate data, victim surveys, and, more typically, offenders' vivid descriptions of their daily lifestyles, choices, and predatory behaviors. Although research has given uneven treatment to victims' descriptions and experiences, offenders' accounts of their crimes and victims contribute to a growing and important body of literature. From it, we learn of, among other things, target selection, decision-making, offenders' efforts at generating compliance, neutralization techniques, and the logistical requisites for engaging repetitively in property crimes (Luckenbill 1981; Bennett and Wright 1984; Honaker 1990; Tunnell 1992; Wright and Decker 1994; 1997; Shover 1996; Hochstetler 2001; Bernasco and Luykx 2003).

TARGET SELECTION

Target selection has been the subject of great interest and research over the past two or three decades. Research to date has used samples of both former repeat offenders and currently and highly active property offenders. Offenders have given their views on private dwellings, businesses, and individuals as potential targets for burglaries and armed robberies (Bennett and Wright 1984; Wright and Decker 1994; 1997). From this body of research, one consistent theme is that as offenders select a target "they are under the influence of two seemingly conflicting demands: one calling for immediate action, and the other counseling caution" (Wright and Decker 1994, 62). Victims are caught in the confluence as these two interests are reconciled in action.

While seeking out lucrative targets, offenders typically move within their awareness space and hence rarely cross class or racial neighborhood lines. Recent interview research with active, urban, armed robbers shows that the majority of their victims share similar characteristics with the offenders; each lives within the inner city, is nonwhite and poor. Robbers typically select targets for crime within or adjacent to their neighborhoods, indicating some reluctance about venturing far from their home, community, and awareness space. Reasons given for their aversion to committing crimes elsewhere include the belief that traveling back to their neighborhoods afterward presents too great a risk; their need for immediate cash and selecting easily accessible targets; and their perceptions that neighborhoods other than their own, and especially white affluent suburbs (as opposed to almost completely poor, nonwhite urban areas), are subjectively out of the realm of target possibilities. White affluent neighborhoods typically are in the county or suburbs and are often gated. When asked about their reluctance to victimize affluent areas, offenders describe "the county as if it were a land of forbidden fruits; a place chock full of tempting targets, but also one harboring great dangers for would-be lawbreakers." Offenders express the belief that county residents are much more likely to report suspicious persons or behaviors in their neighborhoods than urban dwellers (Wright and Decker 1997, 74).

Other interview research with persistent burglars reports similarly. Some black offenders, for example, claim that they would not attempt to burgle a home in the more affluent white neighborhoods in part because they believe their presence there would raise suspicions with neighbors and passersby. Some also believe that if apprehended in white affluent neighborhoods, punishment, in terms of a prison sentence, would be more severe than for similar crimes in poor and/or minority neighborhoods (Private interview 1988). From research to date, repeat offenders typically claim that the least risky areas for engaging in property crimes are those within or those immediately adjacent to their own neighborhoods (Tunnell 1992; Wright and Decker 1997; Bernasco and Luykx 2003).

Offenders report that particular victims are defined as suitable, in fact, appealing targets because they are involved in some form of illegality, most commonly vice crimes. For example, offenders burgle the homes of drug dealers because of the large sums of cash and drugs on hand and the realization that these victims, unlike noncriminal ones, will not report the crime to the police. Similarly, some armed robbers stick-up drug dealers, bootleggers, players in high-stakes card games, and places of vice activity for the same reasons—the rewards are plentiful and the risks of official intervention are nil (Tunnell 1992; Wright and Decker 1994; 1997; Jacobs 2000). The major concern for the offenders in these cases is that victims may personally retaliate. According to recent self-report studies, property offenders have high crime victimization rates providing them with the unique insights of both offenders and victims (Wright and Decker 1997).

Research with active burglars indicates that there is some semblance of calculation taking place regarding target selection, potential pay offs, and potential risks and their severity. From self-report data, but using hypothetical situations, burglars claim that they respond to the threat of sanctions regarding both the likelihood of such and the amount (e.g., the number of years in prison). In cases when the sanction threat is high, burglars claim they are less willing to view the target as suitable. When burglars view the target as likely to produce a pay-off with few risks, they claim they are more likely to define it as suitable. From small samples, using hypothetical situations, there is some support for rational choice and the efficacy of deterrence (Piquero and Rengert 1999). In the main, however, among chronic property offenders, and especially those with drug addictions and daily needs for cash, rational calculation and planning are the exception rather than the rule (Currie 1985; Tunnell 1992).

VICTIMIZATION AND SOCIAL CLASS

Property crime in America largely is intra-class. Although intra-class crime apparently is the norm, it evidently is not necessarily a working or middle-class phenomenon. Instead, it generally involves one poor person victimizing another. In other words, street crime is an underclass phenomenon. Repetitive property offenders described in recent studies typically commit crimes against poor, working, and middle-class individuals; small businesses; and those involved in illegalities, particularly vice crimes (Wright and Decker 1994; 1997; Tunnell 1992). Their actions are not aimed at the rich, the powerful, state representatives, or others whom they conceivably could hold somewhat accountable for inequalities, the conditions of the poor, their own deprived status, and/or their limited opportunities. Rather, they continually target the powerless and blameless with motivations void of rage, rebellion, or antisystemic anger. Their actions most commonly are intra-class crimes, but bearing little resemblance to the recent concept— "intra-working class crime" (Lowman 1992; DeKeseredy and Schwartz 1996b, 307). Rather, their crimes represent acts of poor against poor, or *underclass crime*. Persistent criminals, as is shown throughout this book, are underclass members.

Previous crime types, for example, whose labels are based on offenders' qualities, include white-collar crime, youth crime, organized crime, political crime, and hate crime, each defined by the offenders' position, characteristics, or motives. Treating crime and victimization as underclass crime follows the sociological tradition of labeling a crime category based on offenders' characteristics.

Although property offenders' crimes occasionally are inter-class, their actions, unlike white-collar, youth, hate, political, and organized crimes, do not victimize people who are worse off financially than they; in fact, there are few individuals worse off. Yet, such acts from the bottom up, which conceivably could be class-driven behaviors containing political meaning, are instead void of group or class motivation and objective. There is little political or romantic about them or their behaviors. Although their actions, to some extent, represent a resistance to legitimate authority, they also are hedonistic and immediately gratifying behaviors, accomplished with little planning and sophistication and with no stated political agenda (as recent Left realist literature also states). Rather, their actions provide expressive rewards and money for sustenance, pleasure, and addictive drugs.

Property crimes that are interclass nearly always victimize one from a higher strata. When street criminals victimize someone of another class, it usually is an upwardly projected offense. Corporate criminals, on the other hand, victimize those below. Some exceptional property offenders do, however, prey regularly on members of higher social classes. For example, some burgle "mansions" and others report that they have broken into "lucrative" homes with "the aid of an insurance agent" (Wright and Decker 1994, 75). Although in these cases victims were selected because offenders defined their homes as containing "good stuff," their cues about target selection were based on a subjective judgment. Such evaluations are based on "the poor housing conditions in which a majority of the offenders found themselves living and in light of the realistically available alternatives" (Wright and Decker 1994, 81). In other words, a class-based evaluation, from the perspective of the relatively deprived offender, was at work.

Although other classes are victimized by repetitive property criminals, such interclass victimization occurs far less frequently than intra-class victimization. In most cases, poor victims and offenders converge within areas characterized by their meager and subsidized housing, few employment opportunities, high unemployment levels, and schools that cannot compete with those found in affluent neighborhoods. As a result, victimization is not an entirely random event. Criminal victimization is most often linked to lifestyle, routine activities, situations linked to particular space, and such aggregate phenomena as class, race, age, and gender.

The point is that victims and offenders converge on the streets of familiar neighborhoods as armed robbers and burglars select their targets. Whether we refer to explanations for these events as situational, lifestyle, or routine activities approaches, the common denominator, or the essence of just what is taking place, is life. People are simply living their lives within strictured neighborhoods without the options, privileges, and security enjoyed in middle-class or affluent communities. Living their lives means that poor residents will likely encounter poor criminals who, at some point, may define them and their property as suitable targets for theft.

In public dialogues, at least, victims most often are presented as blameless and criminals as individual deviants. In each case, the social is too often ignored. This commonly described victim–offender dichotomy does not accurately portray the complexities of crime and especially underclass crime committed by repeat offenders typically within socially disorganized neighborhoods.

Evidence shows too that some victims are selected deliberately as a means by which to avenge a perceived wrong or as "self-help." After all, there are situations where some offenders and victims are "participants in a dynamic, ongoing interaction." Roles may shift as the actors, at any given moment, can be considered victim or offender, "depending on the stage of the interaction. For instance, in an ongoing relationship, one of the actors may be taking retribution . . . on the other actor for an earlier victimization" (McShane and Williams 1992, 261). Consider actors' implicit agreement to escalate a tense situation (such as a barroom brawl) and produce a violent outcome. Either party may emerge as offender or victim (Luckenbill 1977). In these cases, one function of the criminal justice system is to apply the labels *criminal* and *victim* when oftentimes such labels could apply to either party. The arbitrariness of imposing a master status is evident in these systemic machinations.

John Hagan and Ruth Peterson (1995, 23; also referring to Black 1984) suggest "some crime in minority neighborhoods may be a product of retaliation" or self-help and "in these contexts, the lines between victimization and offending are frequently unclear." Wright and Decker (1994, 59–60) report similarly. They suggest that such acts may involve the pursuit of street justice between two individuals. Their offender-participants reported that burglary was a way to right a perceived wrong, for example, or an attempt to control the influx of particular "outsiders" (those determined to be different) from moving into their neighborhoods. Some offenders, desiring to right a wrong, select and burgle homes of individuals whom they begrudge. Even given these realities, crime for revenge is the exception rather than the rule for understanding victimization chances and trends.

VICTIMOLOGY

At one time, both crime control officials and academics largely ignored crime victims. But the development of victim services has fundamentally transformed the once silent voices of victims into fairly powerful and vocal interest groups. Today, addressing victims' needs and preventing victimization are central components of the expanding and financially lucrative crime control industry as new services and commodities serving crime victims (and those who fear victimization) are in abundance and as legislation accommodates victims and their views on crime and punishment (Newburn and Stanko 1994, 153; Christie 1993; Fattah 1997).

Victimology remains, however, a thorny issue for academics in general and progressive ones in particular. This is due, in part, to the co-optation of victims' rights movements, primarily by conservative, law, and order campaigns supporting centralized punishment strategies (Fattah 1997). As a result, victimology, which in many ways has become an advocate for the state more so than for individual victims, has propagated images that have served the interests of conservative crime control strategies and strengthened state powers (McShane and Williams 1992, 259).

One function of victimology has been its contribution to order maintenance by supporting the criminal justice system as that entity best able to resolve disputes. Victimology's reticence to move beyond incomplete mediated images often results in its remaining an advocate for the state and private and political interests (McShane and Williams 1992). Victimology's focus is almost solely on garden-variety crimes and affirms skewed media depictions of the criminal and victim.

While fear of crime runs rampant and victims' interest movements support increasing punitiveness, fear of the other varies across groups. The young, the poor, the nonwhite, and women are suspected of a number of deviant activities. The suspicion is often based on openly displayed subcultural traits and styles rather than criminal or threatening behavior (see, e.g., Ferrell 1995). Safety has become such an immense concern that efforts made to ward off those defined as potential criminals spread "the safety fears further, for example to gangsta rap, male teenage dress codes, adolescent swagger, and other lifestyles of the poor, all diverging ever more from those of the adult mainstream" (Gans 1995, 80). Victimology, unfortunately, has defended suspicions of the other as one strategy in its concern for preventing further vicimization.

Critical sociology (excepting Left realism) has been relatively silent on the victim issue. This silence is due to a variety of reasons. First, commentaries on victimization have been unsettling for critical social science. These issues have been supported mostly by parties supporting extending the powers and increasing the punishments of the crime control industry. As a result, a vitally important and human-centered issue, such as addressing crime victims' needs, has been co-opted by the political Right. Academics, and especially critical ones, are too often left on the sidelines.

Second, while victims' needs and rights have received redress by systems managers (prosecutors, judges, advocacy groups, etc.), other components of the crime equation have had little vocal support. Consider, for example, the attention in the form of rhetoric and legislation given to (or in the name of) victims compared to that given to rehabilitation efforts of offenders; investments in early crime prevention, such as education and after school programs; investments in inner cities; access to reasonably priced drugs, methadone, and needle-exchange programs; social welfare programs; real job training for the poor; addressing discrimination against ethnic minorities and the poor; demilitarizing the police; restorative justice; and communitarian adjudication programs (see, e.g., Rodriguez 2005; Cullen 2005). None of these has received the attention that victims' rights and advocacy movements obtained by systems managers and political officials (although, as Francis Cullen 2005 shows, the body of evidence supports rehabilitation efforts). As a result, issues that are just as important as victimization have largely been treated as less important, leaving some in the social sciences with few human-centered crime control policies to support. This is especially the case given that victims' rights has been so openly embraced by the political Right and nonacademic interest groups.

Third, victims' movements often present the conflict that produces personal victimization between offender and society rather than between two humans caught in a power struggle. This worldview allows little room for restorative justice to prevail (Braithwaite 1994; Cordella 1996). As a result, punishment, rather than healing, is the driving force for victims' redress.

The irony is that the evidence consistently shows that property crime victims rarely desire vengeance or punishment; they prefer restitution. They simply want their property replaced, repaired, or returned (Fattah 1997).

At one time, as critics have long claimed, victimology treated victims as precipitators in their own victimization. Now critics claim that victimology conceptualizes and treats victims as purely innocents, with little experience in or knowledge of crime, victimization prevention strategies, or understanding crime's real threat to themselves and their property (Newburn and Stanko 1994, 154).

Despite advances in victimology, little is known, for example, of men's victimization. This is largely due to widely held (yet untested) beliefs that masculinity hinders men from revealing the details of their own victimizations (Newburn and Stanko 1994, chap. 9). Victim research has also focused much more on urban crime and victimization patterns than on rural ones. Simply applying what we know about urban crime and victimization to the rural experience is inappropriate. Victimization and crime are quite different in the countryside than in the city.

Feminist scholarship, which has advanced our knowledge of victims, has never had much appreciation for the lifestyle approach for explaining victimization. The approach allegedly ignores power differentials by gender and does not account for the violence experienced most by women—that within the household. Recently, Left realism, with victimization as its central plank, has gained support from feminists, but not without criticism. Realism generally accepts state definitions of crime and fails to "incorporate fully an understanding of power relationships into its theoretical framework" (Newburn and Stanko 1994, 157).

According to Stanley Cohen (1993, 100), only radical victimology "extends to all forms of human suffering and sees law and the criminal justice system as implicated in this suffering." This is, to some extent, contrary to Left realism, which accepts the traditional role of the criminal justice system in resolving legal conflicts (although, to be fair, realism supports decentralized crime control measures). Realism, accusing idealism of romanticizing criminals as potentially rebellious antisystemic individuals, has likewise been charged with romanticizing working-class victims. Idealism is accused of romanticizing the criminal, while realism may romanticize the victim.

From these disparate interpretations, the image of crime and victimization is skewed. Also, from these different schools of thought, little emerges that highlights the participation of otherwise noncriminal individuals in reproducing property crime and victimization. That is the subject of the next section.

THE PERVASIVENESS OF CRIME THROUGH
UNDERGROUND ECONOMIES

Property crime is deeply entrenched in American culture. It is financially viable in part because a mutually beneficial relationship exists between property offenders and the otherwise law-abiding public (many of whom have been victims at one time or another). Armed robbery, the most serious yet least frequently occurring property crime, provides the assailant with instant cash. But the most frequently occurring crimes of theft are those where property rather than money is stolen. Stolen goods must be converted into legal tender since few property offenders have need for, say, a dozen television sets or handguns. This is where the law-abiding public, through various subterranean economies, supports and, like the property offenders themselves, profits from crimes of theft.

Research on this issue clearly distinguishes the general public as occasional buyers of stolen goods from professional fences (Hall 1952; Klockars 1974). The former buys goods primarily for their own personal use, while the latter maintains ongoing professional relationships with property criminals through mutually beneficial profit-making campaigns. Fences, however, in the end, sell their newly acquired wares to the general public, although often to an unsuspecting rather than a willing public. Stolen automobiles, for example, are often chopped or stripped of their parts that end up in repair shops and ultimately in savvy shoppers' cars.

Paul Cromwell, James Olson, and D'Aunn Wester Avary (1991, 72), for example, report that their sample of burglars sold a "significant proportion of property stolen" directly to the public for their own personal use or for resale. In fact 58 percent reportedly sold stolen items to individuals rather than to professional fences. This study indicates that the public plays a role in maintaining property crime.

Sellers of stolen merchandise are commonly encountered in cities and suburbia, on street corners, in shopping centers, in parking lots, and in a host of other places where potential buyers are found. In more rural areas, stolen goods are often sold at flea markets, yard sales, auctions, and in various trade publications. Stuart Henry (1978, 12), describing this part of the underground economy, claims that the distinction between honest and dishonest is artificial, and it "masks the fact that the hidden economy is the on-the-side, illegal activity of 'honest' people who have legitimate jobs and who would never admit being dishonest." Thus, honest people who buy stolen goods (admittedly often in naïve ignorance) in part subsidize the activities of street criminals. Likewise, honest people subsidize the activities of white-collar offenders as the costs of their crimes are passed along to consumers, workers, stockholders, and taxpayers.

Consumers desire good deals and inexpensively priced items, whether that means a hot television or cheap clothing legally manufactured by Third World prisoners and children. Casual buyers of stolen goods, like the criminals themselves, are able to neutralize guilt, negative feelings, and their desire to continue buying stolen property. They are able to do so, for example, by cognitively redefining it as a good bargain and a widely engaged in behavior (Cromwell et al. 1991, 76). Also, they are able to deny the likelihood that the goods they purchase are stolen. Neutralization techniques are used by property offenders as well as sellers and buyers of stolen goods.

Although no one particularly relishes placing blame on the general public for crime and victim problems, we cannot ignore entrenched financial arrangements, systems, and organizations that allow otherwise law-abiding individuals to gain from victimization. Buying and selling stolen goods is engrained in specific ways of doing business and in consumers' quest for a good bargain. Consumers and consumer demand are part of the equation that guarantees that crimes of theft will continue and that repeat offenders will persist in their daily or near daily illegalities.

6

EXPLAINING REPETITIVE PROPERTY CRIME

Repetitive property offenders, like other groups across history, have been labeled a "problem population." If self-report estimates of criminal activity are close to accurate, then repeat criminals, as a group, are responsible for stealing enormous sums from individuals and businesses. The label, *problem population*, then, as applied to this group, may be accurate. Labeling, however, compounds the problems for those publicly designated as problematic, for society's response to them and their activities, and for teasing out subtle back- and foreground characteristics of their criminal histories (see Paternoster and Iovanni 1985 for a review of the extant literature). Nonetheless, the label, as applied to this group, is an apt description and is widely used.

Theoretical and empirical explanations abound for the problem population of highly active property offenders. Each theory has its own degree of explanatory power and brings useful insights to the topic. Public strategies for how best to respond to repetitive offenders are unfortunately too often uninformed by research. They are also highly politicized and often inadvertently dysfunctional.

Given the diffuse sociological and criminological explanations, general theories of crime have been advanced (Gottfredson and Hirschi 1990; Tittle 1995; Akers 1998). With competing general theories, recent attempts have been made at theory integration (Barak 1998). These integrations and theories are unique in their ability to synthesize explications and to account for various types of crime. Although none is universally applicable, each has advanced theoretical sophistication and offers promise for new ways of thinking theoretically.

While efforts have been made at integration or general theoretical explanations, other offerings are intentionally fragmented or disjointed.

Human behavior, so the argument goes, is too complex, multilayered in its meaning, situationally constructed, dynamic, and too little understood to fit within general or integrationist theories.

Expressing reluctance at accepting one theoretical explanation (or general theory) for crime, anarchist criminology, for example, rejects master plans—including its own. Rather, it "embraces instead fluid communities of uncertainty and critique" as a stance against a single explanation, the rule of law, the widening net of social control, and coercive and punitive policies (Ferrell 1997, 152).

Judging from the academic literature, specific, localized, theoretical explanations are preferred over master plans. There is support as well for community generated and implemented policies for dealing with crime rather than centralized plans that emphasize highly rationalized and bureaucratic policing, crime control, and punitive strategies.

As argued throughout this book, social class has long been central to theoretical explanations of property crimes and criminals. Numerous theories with different levels of explanation and implicit ideology use class to highlight the social problem of crime. Given this history, the following sections give brief coverage to theories that treat class as central to their explications (or that infer the relevance of class to the crime problem) and that intimate public strategies for how best to respond to the predatory crime problem. Left realism, social ecology, and strain theories are important to these issues. Social learning theory that links behavior to social structure (and implicitly economics and social class) also has a great deal to contribute to the discussion of predatory crime. Each is useful for understanding repeat property offenders, their crimes, and informed social policies. As is shown below, some components offer more than others.

LEFT REALISM

Left realism emerged as both a response to Left idealism and to the growing crime problems faced largely by urban, working, and underclass neighborhoods. These oft-neglected communities, some of which are painfully impacted by predatory crimes and criminals, were of primary concern to early developments within Left realism. Realism claims to offer some balance to ongoing academic and public policy responses to crime that (according to realism, yet few others) had neglected the importance of working-class crime by giving priority to crimes among the powerful (that is to say, corporate and governmental misdeeds) (Lowman 1992).

Left realism's explanation, since its inception, has included strategies for containing crime. Since Left realism is part theory and part policy, any discussion of it, by necessity, includes both. Realism offers the "square of crime"—the offender, victim, state, and public—as a central component of its theoretical explanation. Less a theory than a loose set of positions for research and short-term, progressive solutions to the street crime problem, the square of crime attempts a macro-micro link with Marxism, victimology, strain, subcultural, and ecological theories (Young 1992a; DeKeseredy, MacLean, and Schwartz 1997). The state and its agencies of control, in the tradition of Foucault, are placed at the center and are ambiguous rather than entirely negatively coercive forces (Matthews and Young 1992).

Regarding the etiology of predatory crime, Left realism highlights connections among social structure and criminal behavior. Class is linked to predatory crime especially within communities with concentrated poverty (Matthews and Young 1992; Young 1992a). Realism also emphasizes that predatory crime is intra-racial, a point supported by victims' and offenders' self-reporting. The more commonly occurring crimes of theft are also mostly intra-racial and intra-class. Familiarity with neighborhoods, offenders' awareness space, neighborhoods' social disorganization, neighborhood segregation, and, to some extent, offenders' realization of the racism and class bias within the criminal justice system account for criminals' preying mostly on individuals of their own race and social class (Tunnell 1992; Wright and Decker 1994; 1997). Realism's focus, like that of most crime research, is on urban issues. Research is scant on crime and victimization patterns among suburban and rural people of color and "the invisible poor" (Harrington 1962; Weisheit et al. 1999).

Since realism treats crime as intra-class, it claims that the working class fears street crime more than white-collar crime. As a result, street crime, more than others, deserves attention. Yet, all classes fear street crime more than white-collar crime. This is no accident. The dominant image of crime in North America, and in various parts of Western Europe, is random, violent, predatory crime. Far from accurate, it is a mediated image reproduced by politicians and law enforcement and left largely unchallenged by the near-absence of academic voices in the mass media (Barak 1988).

One area deserving of attention is the processes by which fears of particular types of crime and criminals are socially constructed and reproduced. Understanding how images are disseminated and internalized, and how they compare to the empirical realities, are also important (see, e.g., Gusfield 1963; K. Wright 1985; Goode and Ben-Yehuda 1994).

As realism reminds us, people's concerns about crime and victimization should not simply be dismissed. Given the social construction of crime news, however, their concerns also should not simply be accepted. Realism's concern with street crime and the fears that it engenders is an important reminder—both theoretically and empirically—that throngs of people in poor, disorganized neighborhoods live with the daily realities of predatory, intra-class behavior.

Related to social class is realism's position that relative deprivation rather than poverty (actually, *absolute poverty*) explains more about crime and criminals. Granted, few offenders (other than the homeless who participate primarily in minor offenses) experience absolute poverty. Nearly no one in North America lives in absolute poverty, although some of the twelve million children living in poverty in the United States do reportedly go to bed hungry (Mangum et al. 2003; O'Hare and Johnson 2004). The distinctions drawn between relative deprivation and poverty are given further attention in the following paragraphs.

Michael Harrington's widely influential book, *The Other America* (1962), described the issue of persistent poverty in the United States. It called attention to and raised a nation's consciousness about the "invisible poor" in both rural and urban areas. Harrington's book, more so than any other publication in its day, helped shape national policy. Soon after its publication, Washington, D.C., declared a "war" on poverty that was intended not only to cure the poverty problem but, according to then-President Johnson, "prevent it." Forty years afterward, there are more poor people and more poor families in the United States than when the war began. The national poverty rate has fluctuated since the early 1960s from a high of 22.4 percent to a low of 11.1 percent (about 25 million people) in 1973. Since then, it has varied from 15.1 percent in the early 1990s to 11.3 percent (about 34 million) in 2000. The rate has never fallen below the 1973 low mark, leaving the United States with the highest poverty rate of all developed countries (Mangum et al. 2003).

The poverty line or threshold, although an important measure, does not reveal the extent of people's experienced poverty. Rather, the *poverty gap*—the difference between the poverty line and actual family income of the poor—is often used as an indicator of the extent of *lived* poverty. Although narrowing at the onset of the war on poverty, the poverty gap has widened since 1967. And, although the poverty rate is lower today than in 1967, the poor experience poverty that "is deeper than in the past," indicating "the existence of a hard core of poor persons who remain resistant to antipoverty efforts while others move in and out of the poverty ranks"

(Mangum et al. 2003, 7). It is this hard-core group of poor people, some of which are repeat offenders, that comprises a chronic underclass in America.

The poverty threshold, first introduced in the mid-1960s, is a figure that is "one-half the median post-tax income for four-person families." This official poverty measure, based on food costs, is characterized as "an absolute measure of poverty." The other indicator, one's earnings relative to median post-tax income, is characterized as "relative poverty" (Mangum et al. 2003, 8 and 9). American families increased in number from 45 million to 72 million across the forty years of the war on poverty. Whether using an absolute or a relative definition of poverty, "the numbers and rates of family poverty in the United States were higher in 1999 than they were in 1973," when rates dropped to their low point a decade after the beginning of official antipoverty reforms (Mangum et al. 2003, 10). As a result, there are far more families living in poverty today than just before the war was declared (15.8 million in 1999 compared to 9.1 million in 1959).

Chronic offenders are poor by almost any definition. Their earnings generally are at or below the official poverty threshold (fixed at $8,959 for one person in 2000). They are counted as poor by their governments. They and their families often receive benefits reserved for the poor. Some are products of multigenerational poverty, and, because of it, they have experienced a different quality of life than others. It is well documented that the poor, and especially those who were poor in their childhood, have a lower quality of life and have a shorter life expectancy than the nonpoor. They suffer in academic and educational achievements. They suffer from poor health care. They are more likely to have conduct problems in school, to repeat grades, and to drop out of school altogether, and they are more likely to have contact with the criminal justice system. These characteristics often precede delinquent behavior, adolescent parenthood, joblessness, and infrequent employment in adulthood. Many poor children become poor adults with little social capital, education, and participation in the labor market—the recipe for producing another generation of poor children and continuing a multigenerational "cycle of poverty" (Mangum et al. 2003, 14).

The state of being relatively deprived is a comparative measure of one's own situation to that of others. Members of each class (except the elite of the elite) may experience some sense of relative deprivation when comparing their economic situations to those above them. Yet, the majority of people do not commit crime even when realizing their situation is worse than others or when things seem unfair. Poor and working-class members, like those of other classes, in the main are law-abiding. Relative deprivation may exist within most classes, but, as Left realism reminds us, it is inseparable from the poor and their perceptions of their situations relative to others. Thus, it is not simply a matter of poverty. It likewise is not only a matter of relative deprivation. Rather, it is deprivation at a certain level of being deprived. It is not simply a factor of relative deprivation but excessive deprivation, a state of far greater deprivation than that experienced by members of other classes. The poor, by definition, experience relative deprivation like no other class.

That repeat property offenders come from the ranks of the poor is important because social class location often determines cultural values. Focal concerns often displayed by poor males, for example, reflect their impoverished class (Miller 1958). Class location determines their worldview and their possibilities, both legal and illegal (see, e.g., Cloward and Ohlin 1960). Both poverty and relative deprivation are important for explaining continual participation in property crime. Underclass criminals are shaped by the values of a market society and the cultural importance given to consumption. They, like their law-abiding underclass counterparts, own little and are unable to participate in conspicuous consumption. Property offenders, however, opt for illegal actions that bring them immediate gratification and instant access to the marketplace.

The issue of relative deprivation within market societies and offenders' decisions to remedy their deprivation through criminal actions are relevant to strain theory (which is discussed later in this chapter).

SOCIAL ECOLOGY AND PERSISTENT CRIME

Social ecology theories have their roots in the early to mid-twentieth-century Chicago School. Social disorganization, a long-standing central explanation within the social ecology tradition, remains highly relevant to explanations of contemporary social problems. Social disorganization refers to communities that are characterized by their inability "to realize the common values of their residents or solve commonly experienced problems" (Bursik 1988, 521). Disorganized communities' commonly experienced problems include high rates of poverty, predatory crimes, infant mortality, juvenile delinquency, and mental illness.

The social disorganization thesis points to three specific community indicators that contribute to above average crime rates: low economic status and poor living conditions, high levels of population turnover, and ethnic heterogeneity. Areas with low economic status or class are more likely to experience high levels of in- and out-migration and ethnic heterogeneity, which contribute to community disorganization. Given such grave differences between people and their lack of commitment to their communities, residents are unlikely to know one another, to care to know one another, to involve themselves in neighborhood activities or organizations, to supervise their or their neighbors' children, or to stay informed of community activities. As a result, there is little interaction among residents, little informal monitoring of others' behavior (whether legal or illegal), and a weakening of primary social relationships and the social bond. Informal social controls found in more stable neighborhoods do not function adequately in disorganized communities.

More recently, neighborhoods have become less heterogeneous than during the early period of social ecology theories. Poverty and mobility, however, remain relevant to the social disorganization of communities experiencing large numbers of single-parent families, multiple rental units and housing projects, gentrification, and a growing urban underclass that is chronically unemployed and that possesses few marketable skills.

Community social disorganization may also result from official state policies aimed at controlling crime, containing offenders, and selectively incapacitating them. Offenders, it is argued, have complex relationships to their many networks within their communities. Their participation has both positive and negative consequences for family and community. When arrested and incarcerated, "their removal in large numbers alters those networks both positively and negatively" (Rose and Clear 1998, 442). Within communities that are disorganized, this removal, as official state policy, may "damage neighborhood structure by disrupting network ties of offenders and nonoffenders and fostering alienation among residents and between the neighborhood and the state" (Rose and Clear 1998, 442). Thus, the argument is that increasing dependence on formal control methods may hinder communities' ability to foster other, less-formal control measures and may result in more, not less, social disorganization (Rose and Clear 1998, 443).

Communities that are socially disorganized are further impacted by their lack of collective efficacy. Collective efficacy, as stated earlier in the book, refers to trust among neighbors "combined with a willingness to intervene on behalf of the common good, specifically to supervise children and maintain public order" (Sampson, Raudenbush, and Earls 1998, 1). As neighborhoods experience increasing social disorganization, they typically experience declining collective efficacy. The social ecology thesis is centered on structural forces that give rise to criminogenic places, classes of people, and opportunities for illegal behavior.

Criminology continues to explain linkages between structure and agency and opportunity and choice. Recent explications place class at their core. They describe structural changes within the United States and particularly within disorganized metropolitan centers. Such changes are apropos for understanding both the state of the underclass and property crime in depressed urban areas (Hagan 1994, chap. 3). The changes experienced by some cities include capital disinvestment, out-migration of working- and middle-class families, ongoing residential segregation by race, racial inequality, and the concentration of poverty within increasingly segregated areas. Not coincidentally, these same communities have witnessed increases in vice service industries and criminal subcultures operating within underground economies. Furthermore, world changes regarding technology, trade, the global economy, domestic relations, and tax and welfare policies have adversely impacted cities and their poor communities.

These explanations focus on recent sociopolitical and economic modifications that have occurred over the past quarter century and that have adversely impacted myriad communities. These changes explain, in part, the high concentrations of property crime within particular communities and their residents' limited legitimate choices and lack of collective efficacy.

This social disorganization explanation highlights social changes that have occurred on a global scale and their impact on communities and their members. Global changes are relevant to economic and political factors that impact young people, neighborhoods, and crime. For example, in the United States, the golden age (ca. 1954–1974) ended with an economic slowdown. From 1974 to the present, economic growth decreased by half to 2.5 percent yearly, while economic inequality increased and reductions in gender inequality slowed. The last half of the twentieth century witnessed capital and job flight and increasing inequalities. Economic growth slowed and opportunities declined. During that time, the poorest women and minorities, more than others, experienced sharp declines in real wages. Job losses, especially in the rust belt manufacturing industries, occurred en masse. The industrial age in the United States was ending as the service sector economy, relying on part-time, low-paying jobs, was growing (Hagan 1994). Such changes and their effects on individuals' life chances and crime are exemplified by the following words from an active armed robber who personally was affected by the downturn in the industrial sector and whose crimes, in part, were determined by these forces:

> My desire is to be gainfully employed in the right kind of job. If I had a
> union job making sixteen or seventeen dollars an hour, something that I
> could really take care of my family with, I think that I could become

cool with that. Years ago I worked at one of the local car factories; I really wanted to be in there. It was the kind of job I'd been looking for. Unfortunately, as soon as I got in there they had a big layoff (Wright and Decker 1997, 48).

During the period of economic decline of the late twentieth century, the United States witnessed three major disinvestment processes that discouraged the growth of social capital within some communities: residential segregation, race-linked inequality, and concentrations and, as Wilson (1987) has shown, the concentration effects of poverty. Since the mid-1970s, concentrated poverty and unemployment have increased especially in older urban centers of the United States. Research, using a variety of methods, continues showing the effects of disinvestment on the communities of, for example, New York, Northwest Chicago, East Los Angeles, Milwaukee, and Kenosha (Wisconsin) (Wilson 1987; Hagedorn 1988; Sullivan 1989; Dudley 1994). Each of these community-based studies highlights the disinvestment experienced by them and the accompanying rise of social problems, concentrated poverty, underground economies, and crime. The Michael Moore film, *Roger and Me* (1989), highlighted similar effects on the city of Flint, Michigan.

Recent history indicates that whenever disinvestment occurs in communities, it is often met with recapitalization (i.e., an effort to reorganize what few resources remain). These measures often include subterranean and illegal activities (such as vice service centers and other underground economies) where growing numbers of predators and prey meet within depressed and hardened urban neighborhoods.

Socially disorganized communities have disproportionately high populations of street criminals and victims. Illegal activities often thrive in those areas that come to be known for gambling, prostitution, and dealing in drugs, guns, and stolen property. Activities there are often supported by violence at least until the illegitimate businesses become integrated within the community (see, e.g., Cloward and Ohlin 1960).

This explanation within the social ecology tradition, gives great attention to the political economy of community, crime, growing numbers of disenfranchised individuals, and the rise of economically viable criminal enterprises dealing in vice and stolen property. The focus on political-economic changes and their impact shifts attention away from individuals per se to structural forces on communities and their skewed social classes, within which are found persistent offenders.

STRAIN THEORY

Strain theory, most often credited to Robert Merton, is central to discussions of underclass repetitive property offenders. Class, poverty, inequality, and relative deprivation are implicitly a part of strain theory. Robert Merton (1957), expanding Emile Durkheim's (1897/1951) notion of anomie by focusing especially on anomic societies, applied his explication directly to the U.S. experience. Since his writing, others, most notably, Steven Messner and Richard Rosenfeld (2001), have continued applying strain theory to an American-style capitalism that features entrenched poverty and deprivation.

Strain theory's focus is structural, but it describes the process by which individuals (and groups) respond and adapt to particular social structures. For strain theory, some societies, by the very nature of their structure, are criminogenic. The assumption, then, is that some societies are organized *for* crime. For strain theory, the old adage that "societies get the type and amount of crime that they deserve," is an apt one. Strain theory recognizes that some societies are more polarized than others. The United States has a highly unequal socioeconomic structure characterized by persistently widening wealth and income gaps. This social structure, of course, also affects the quantity and quality of power and social capital; it produces privilege but also entrenched poverty. According to the U.S. Census Bureau, for example, there currently are 40 million Americans (or nearly one-fifth of the U.S. population) living below the poverty threshold. These are people who have been disenfranchised, in part, because of inequalities within the social structure. This economic fact is but one indication of an anomic society.

Merton wrote about the socially approved goals of American society that are highly skewed toward wealth, income, capital, property, and privilege. These goals are widely recognized and accepted by society's members due to socialization, mediated messages, and stated social expectations. Merton's appraisal of American society, however, highlights the reality that socially acceptable opportunities for acquiring socially approved goals are differentially distributed. In other words, some have greater access to obtaining those goals than others—further evidence of an anomic society. This disjuncture between socially approved goals and socially acceptable means to the goals produces strain as people, recognizing the inequities, attempt to adapt to a social structure over which they have little control. Although the majority of people (whether rich or poor) simply accept the realities of an unfair social system and adapt by conforming, such a system also produces deviant and criminal adaptations. Thus, the social structure is said to be criminogenic. This structure then produces property and white-collar crimes as some underclass and corporate-class members adjust by ignoring socially acceptable means to attain socially approved goals.

Although Merton discussed the theory in relation to the American experience, Messner and Rosenfeld (2001) use strain theory with an unprecedented level of specificity. Their discussion characterizes the very structure and culture of American society as anomic and criminogenic. Using a comparative and historical analysis, they show that the United States has exceptionally high levels of crime. With a focus on robbery (as well as murder), their data show that the United States has far higher rates than other industrialized nations. Although America's crime rates declined in the latter part of the twentieth century, they remain higher than rates during the peaks of the late 1960s and early 1970s. Beyond these most serious Index Crimes, the United States also has high levels of white-collar crime.

These consistently high rates that persist over time, Messner and Rosenfeld (2001) suggest, are due to particular enduring patterns of social and cultural organization. These patterns are unique to American-style capitalism. Their argument is that the problem is not capitalism per se, but rather *American* capitalism, a different breed than that found in Western Europe, for example, or the United Kingdom. Their historical interpretation is germane to this issue.

Capitalism evolved in old countries as earlier economies gave way to this new mode of production. The transition, far from smooth, nonetheless was gradual. Cultures changed yet maintained some qualities of previous ways of manufacturing and distributing goods and services. The United States has had only one form of production—capitalism—that highly values individualism. It is a proud, smug version of capitalism and one that has little use for other modes of production. American culture was shaped by this single mode of production; it reflects not only the entrepreneurial spirit of capitalism but also its mean side as well. It values individualism. It rewards individual accomplishments and punishes individual defeats. Its focus for explaining the social is typically reduced to micro-explanations that fail to take into account the complexities of social life, social organization, and a social culture greatly shaped by its singular style of doing business. Unlike other capitalist countries that invest heavily in its people's welfare, *American* capitalism operates in a far more laissez faire manner. It accepts the premise that the economic system works best when left alone. Granted, certain components of U.S. society are socialized and regulated by government, but the unique culture and history of a single economic system have given rise to unique values and traits. These values are embodied in the well-known cultural expression "The American Dream," which signifies a system that allows for the acquisition of wealth and material possessions. This culture also produces problems resulting from the American dream, including property and white-collar crimes. This recent explication of Strain theory argues that America is organized *for* crime because the American dream overemphasizes materialism and economics at the expense of other features of social life.

Messner and Rosenfeld's (2001) argument is that social institutions in America, unlike those of European capitalist countries, are dominated by one single institution—the economy. Although social institutions greatly impact each other in France and Germany, for example, in the United States, they mostly are subject to the whims of the market and those who manage it. In America, nothing is considered as important as the economy. Politics, the family, education, the legal system—each is subservient to the economy. Each serves the economy. American culture, like education or the criminal justice system, is also impacted by the economy (c.f., Reiman 1979).

There arguably is an overemphasis on continual economic growth, individualism, the American Dream, and material acquisition. Material possession is indicative of success. Using Merton's interpretation of anomie, Messner and Rosenfeld (2001) argue that American society is anomic. Despite governmental intervention (e.g., the war on poverty), American economic structure has been consistently characterized by its substantial inequality. It systemically produces ongoing and deeply entrenched patterns of relative poverty and deprivation. This consistency is not an anomaly; it is a pattern that is organizationally and structurally based. Attempts to creatively and structurally address these entrenched problems are not made. Rather, widespread distribution of wealth and income or attempts to address poverty's underlying structural antecedents are viewed as threats to the economy. A society that gives priority to the economy will not tolerate radical efforts. As a result, crime is to be expected in a society with such an emphasis on materialism and individualism but with few socially institutionalized means of attaining economic satisfaction.

Capitalism in America has been referred to as "turbo-charged," and its symptoms are "chronic urban poverty and an exclusionary labor market." Crime in America isn't necessarily due to absolute poverty. It results from "a lethal combination of relative deprivation and individualism . . . [or] poverty experienced as unfair that breeds discontent." This American style capitalism, "takes such discontent to the extremes" (DeKeseredy et al. 2003, 12). This is an important extension of strain theory and one that more clearly connects the crime problem in America to its very structural and cultural organization.

SOCIAL LEARNING THEORY

Linking structure and agency requires an explanation of process or human behavior. Social learning theory's primary focus is on explaining the relationship between the social and the personal since "theories of criminal behavior are neither purely structural nor processual" (Akers 1998, 328).

Differential association-reinforcement theory, an extension of Sutherland's differential association, and an integration of social psychological interactionism with operant behavior, is widely known today as social learning theory (Burgess and Akers 1966; Akers 1985). Social learning theory explains human behavior as that learned through complex conditionings yet within specific social settings and structures which reinforce action.

Ronald Akers's (1998) most recent extension of social learning theory describes the linkages between social structure and agency and is central to discussions of repetitive property crime especially within market societies. For Akers (1985, 45), the social environment is the most important source of reinforcement. Likewise, social interaction, rather than simply one's observations or imitations (although important to this theory), is the process by which deviant and criminal behavior are learned. Thus, for social learning theory, one learns the particular values located within particular social structures, groups, organizations, and subcultures.

American culture is uniquely capitalist and individualist (as Messner and Rosenfeld's main thesis describes) and generally is defined as positive by society's members. Thus, the normative behaviors of acquiring money or material possessions are learned within a particular context and culture that values private ownership and conspicuous consumption. The culture also rewards the acquisition.

Some individuals define crime as a potentially successful method for acquiring money and consuming. According to social learning theory, once definitions are learned, they become a source of stimuli or cues about anticipated consequences of action. These cues can take the form of positive definitions, whereby actors view the behavior as correct and anticipate rewards from action. They also can take the form of negative definitions, whereby actors seek to avoid consequences from particular actions. Definitions also serve to neutralize actions and allow actors to justify or rationalize their behaviors.

> Behavioral theory is based on a response-stimulus-response sequence. That is, operant conditioning (instrumental learning) is a process in which behavior (response) produces consequences (stimuli), and in turn

the recurrence of that behavior is a function of those rewarding or aversive consequences (Akers 1998, 87).

Akers's (1998, 50) concise description of social learning theory is that the "same learning process, operating in a context of social structure, interaction, and situation, produces both conforming and deviant behavior." Central to the learning are the concepts—differential association, differential reinforcement (learning through reward and punishment), imitation, and, as part of the social-psychological tradition, definitions. Whenever the "combined effects of these four main sets of variables instigate and strengthen nonconforming over conforming acts," criminal and deviant behavior are more likely than law-abiding behavior.

Social structure is vital to Akers's explanation of criminal behavior. Edwin Sutherland, whom Akers is indebted to, reminds us that it is social disorganization, or "differential social organization," that affects crime at the aggregate and individual levels. Crime is rooted in the social organization and is an expression of it. Communities, like nations, are organized for and against criminal behavior and crime is a manifestation of that organization (Sutherland 1949). Sutherland connects social organization to differential association. Social learning theory connects social structure and organization to learning criminal and deviant behaviors within social and interactive processes (Akers 1998, chap. 12). One learns within a context where the behavior being learned is valued and in turn reproduced.

Some contexts have greater support for crime and deviance than others. For example, criminal organizations contain more support than, say, the Girl Scouts. Some communities, especially those characterized as disorganized and possessing little collective efficacy, contain more support for crime than stable communities with intimate relationships existing between neighbors. Some countries also have greater support for crime than others. Within these criminogenic social locations, crime is more likely learned than in others. Crime, and crime as a way of life, is theoretically conceptualized as learned behavior within specific contexts supportive of such.

CONCLUSION

One of this book's objectives is to bring class back into the discussion of repetitive property criminals and their subcultures, which value and reproduce their deviant and illegal behaviors. Related to this objective, this book focuses on the growing numbers of underclass individuals and the importance of underclass location to predatory crime and victimization. Although a result of multiple causes, chronic street crime in the United States is related to relative poverty and deprivation and to a growing urban, underclass population.

As central as class is to the property-crime problem, and as central as it perhaps should be to public debates and policies, over the past two decades there has been "staunch intellectual and political opposition to the very idea that crime has much to do with poverty—or with economic conditions generally" (Currie 1996, 40). Nonetheless, the "relationship between poverty and crime is still in existence, regardless of talk to the contrary" by politicians, system managers, and a rather uninformed public (Christie 1981, 60–61). Public strategies and debates about street crime hold little hope as long as they continue ignoring the realities of political-economic strictures of social life. For example,

> The paradox is this: a set of social conditions, of which persistent poverty is a part, has been repeatedly implicated in serious crime and delinquency for decades. Yet it is difficult to find examples of working anticrime strategies that have directly or consistently addressed those conditions (Currie 1996, 37).

The poor, as defined by most Americans and policymakers, are "undeserving" (Gans 1995, 92). Within the criminal justice system, they represent a population that needs to be controlled, policed, monitored, and investigated. Recent crime control policies that contribute to the growth of a crime control industry (and to the over two million people incarcerated in the United States) are directly related to the swelling numbers of poor people (cf., Christie 1993). Countless numbers of jobs, infrastructural commodities, and numerous businesses, all within the crime industrial complex, are increasing due to the growing numbers of poor Americans and the hardened perception of them as undeserving. Their poverty, nonpoor Americans often say, is due to their personal decisions, life choices, and inabilities to engage in long-term goal fulfillment rather than a result of some abstract social structure.

Life in welfare states generally is constructed with safety nets to prevent the poor, or at least the conforming poor, from losing completely. Exceptional individuals, who nonetheless lose most everything, however, are usually good losers. Others, who are not, spend their time retreating or committing crimes. Society's response to them—formal punishment—is often criticized as dubious since preceding conditions are systemically created and, by way of imposing punishment, summarily ignored. For some of those who have lost nearly everything, punishment threats offer little controlling effect (see, e.g., Tunnell 1992, chap. 6). Likewise, informal sanction threats are not particularly foreboding, and the threat of losing work is an empty one since they do not work. "They cannot be controlled by any threat of losing family-relations, they have none. They cannot be controlled by the threat that relatives will suffer; the welfare state is supposed to take care of them" (Christie 1981, 61).

Within the United States, nearly every effort to control or at least contain criminal behavior has been disappointing (unless incarcerating over two million people, as of midyear 2003, indicates success). Evidence empirically connecting any change in criminal behavior or crime trends to government initiative or intervention is, at best, mixed (see, e.g., Steffensmeier and Harper 1999). Some critics allege that state policies have failed because they are myopic rather than radical, psychological rather than structural, punitive rather than peaceful or restorative, and centralized rather than community-based. On the other hand are arguments that imprisonment numbers indicate success in removing predators from society. Contemporary crime control measures have been criticized as "more of the same," and "the least controversial observation about American criminal justice today is that it is remarkably ineffective, absurdly expensive, grossly inhumane, and riddled with discrimination" (Rothman 1995, 29).

The New Penology, concerned with efficiency and less concerned with individuals and causality, focuses on "subgroups or aggregations of individuals and their risks of crime which are to be managed efficiently by means of selective incapacitation through imprisonment" (Hagan 1994, 163). Sentencing reform, mandatory minimum sentences, truth-in-sentencing movements, the war on (some) drugs, selective incapacitation, three strikes and you're out, and political conservatism each has contributed to increased levels of incarceration, especially among poor, nonwhite men and women convicted of (more precisely, plea bargained to) nonviolent crimes.

Justice Department data indicate that 29 percent of new commitments to prison are for violent offenses; 29 percent are for property crimes; 30 percent for drug offenses; and 10 percent for public order offenses. In total, 52 percent of the incarcerated are sentenced for "petty" offenses (operationally defined as actions that do not involve threat of injury, weapon, drugs, and that result in the loss of less than $1,000) (Austin and Irwin 2001). At the federal level, 65 percent of inmates are incarcerated for drug offenses (Federal Bureau of Prisons 2004; Sevigny and Caulkins 2004, 408).

Despite evidence of incarcerating large numbers of low-level and non-violent offenders, alternative crime control measures are little used. Public strategies for preventing and controlling crime and aiding victims in the main are not particularly progressive. Criminology itself has been accused of having lost "interest in criminological depth, and indeed, in criminological truth . . . as [p]ragmatic considerations prompt a return to surface phenomena." The irony within contemporary criminology and crime control initiatives is that these directions and policies that ignore "root causes or deeplying problems [are] not perceived as a failing" (Garland 1995, 194). In part an indictment of sociological criminology for its movement away from critical inquiry and toward policy-relevant research (cf., Braithwaite and Pettit 1990), Bourdieu (1993, 24) likewise reminds us that:

> Like every science, sociology accepts the principle of determinism understood as a form of the principle of sufficient reason. The science which must give the reasons for that which is, thereby postulates that nothing is without a reason for being. The sociologist adds: social reason—nothing is without a specifically social reason for being.

Thus, one objective is to search for social explanations or social reasons for being. This is especially pertinent to the social problem of crime and its control. Social class and its effects on perceptions, motivations, life choices, actions, and victimization risks are relevant.

Less formal methods for containing crime, lessening its impact, and aiding victims have been attempted but, to date, with mixed results. Lance Selva and Robert Bohm (1987) describe the processes by which the informalism experiment in the administration of criminal justice has been co-opted by the internal contradictions and driving forces of bureaucraticization and monopoly capitalism. In a rationalized system, decentralization, moderation, and representation eventually tend to reproduce the very systems that such efforts were designed to change. As a result, even the best efforts put forth by well-intentioned policymakers and systems workers have produced little that is qualitatively different from the tired responses of the past that humanely address victims' rights and offenders' needs (Selva and Bohm 1987). Informal dispute processes, designed to increase communication among the parties, increasingly rely on mediators, yet they often possess scant knowledge of the case. Rather than serving individuals who have been previously excluded from restorative justice, informal dispute processes tend to remove cases from the system, resulting in individuals' further exclusion from all that formal processes have to offer (e.g., funded programs aiding victims' recovery and offenders' treatment). Since most programs are empowered by centralized courts and overseen by professional bureaucrats

and elected officials, evidence suggests that as these informal systems become institutionalized, they take on the very characteristics that they were
designed to circumvent (Selva and Bohm 1987, 49). This critique is reminiscent of Richard Quinney's (1991a) appraisal of our entire history of
crime control—it has been and remains an utter failure, in part, because of
the state's role.

Even restorative justice, which, on its face, offers the informality and
healing absent from current justice practices, has been embraced, to some
extent, by county governments and the Department of Justice (Quinn 1998,
12). Restorative justice, as a model and a concept, holds much promise, yet
with centralized authority, there is less room for optimism than without.

Left Realism, which consistently has shown concern for the crime problem and poor and working-class victims, offers a number of policy sugges-
tions. Realism supports community or "beat" policing and endorses the main
thrust of the "broken windows" thesis that "foot patrol may control minor
crime and that this can stop a spiral of disorganization within a neighborhood" (Young 1992b, 55). Realism supports multiagency responses to crime
and the need "to formulate joint strategies for crime prevention" (Young
1992b; Kinsey, Lea, and Young 1986, 114). One particular strategy advanced
is "colonization," which involves "other institutions in crime prevention . . .
essentially as appendages of the police." A central component of colonization
is a public that feeds "information to the police concerning suspicious circumstances" (Kinsey et al. 1986, 118–19). Granted, this is a crime-prevention
strategy of sorts, however, neighbor ratting on neighbor is hardly a practice
that results in greater community solidarity, autonomy, or mutual support.

Realism also supports "mapping out" trouble spots (Young 1992b;
Lowman and MacLean 1992). While this may appear on the surface as positive for victims and communities, it often does not materialize as such, since
order maintenance policing has become increasingly draconian and nondis-
criminate (e.g., one strike, whether guilty or not, and you're out of U.S.
public housing).

Given its shortcomings, realism, in all fairness, provides some progressive alternatives to conservative, liberal, and Left idealist approaches and offers "middle range policy alternatives" (DeKeseredy and Schwartz 1996b,
307). For example, realism advances further criminalization of acts that
evade the criminal label, such as environmental harms, state crimes, and acts
against women. It also supports a policy of minimalist policing and less than
formal (albeit state-sanctioned) arbitration proceedings.

Although realism continues to have faith in the police and official of-
fices, others maintain that police, courts, and corrections are not very im-

portant to the crime problem (Felson 1994, 8). "When so much crime never comes to the attention of police, we have to begin putting police power and the criminal justice system as a whole into a smaller perspective." After all, the criminal justice system is characterized as an industry that "does everything wrong: It gives punishments rather than rewards and relies on rare and delayed—but extreme—penalties" (Felson 1994, 10).

Writing of crime prevention strategies that are less violent than contemporary neo-classical criminal justice policies, Marcus Felson (1994, 116–17) directs our attention to concepts advanced in earlier work, such as "defensible space," "natural surveillance," "community of interest," and "situational prevention." Suggesting that crime can be prevented in "a practical, natural, and simple way," lessening the crime problem includes "avoiding so far as one can the use of the criminal justice system, armed guards, violence, and threats." Rather, communities should design supportive "situations and environments in which acting legally feels like the normal and comfortable thing to do. . . . It avoids a walled-off society and seeks more sophisticated means for avoiding crime" (Felson 1994, 128).

Criminal justice practice, according to peacemaking and anarchist criminology, is "a violent reaction to, or anticipation of, crime." Rather than restoration, the criminal justice system "is a form of negative peace. Its purpose is to deter or process acts of crime through the threat and application of force" (Quinney 1997, 117). Crime itself and sanctions that follow are harm producing and are "linked to the historical emergence of the formal, rational, centralized state" (Tifft and Sullivan 1980, 118). Peacemaking criminology and anarchism advocate fragmented, community-constructed, peaceful, restorative, reintegrative policies (Braithwaite 1994; Pepinsky 1995). Community building is central to any peacemaking criminology and to the reduction in human suffering.

Anarchism works against state-organized politics of legislating and controlling behaviors (as we know them). A change in dialogue is required from apologist or critical to anarchism's main concern for victims and offenders—gaining freedom from the restraints of government (Goldman 1969, 62)—by adopting Henry Thoreau's (1849/1957, 235) thesis that "government is best which governs not at all." Strategies broadly informed by anarchist perspectives stand against systems of appropriated force, law, and administration, and they stand for new social orders based on freedom from hierarchical and rationalized systems of dominance (Goldman 1967; Tifft and Sullivan 1980, 71–76). These strategies stress the need for dismantling and disrespecting authority rather than reproducing and respecting it. Anarchist strategies seek meaning in the actions of those at the receiving end of authority, that is, those labeled criminal. The stated intention is not to romanticize or reify them and their behaviors, but to understand the moment of action and conflict with authority, its meaning for offenders and victims, and how such is symbolically and politically interpreted and responded to. It also emphasizes the inequities of law, the sheer force of the state in organized policing and coercive conflict resolution, and the state's persistence, which rests squarely on organized and legitimized administration and force (Ferrell 1993, 186–89; Horowitz 1964, 51–53; Kropotkin 1898/1992). Anarchism encourages the ultimate negation of authority while highlighting the necessity of participating in direct action (Ferrell 1993, 191–93; Horowitz 1964, 56).

Anarchism propagates the unlikelihood of a centralized government solving the crime problem or of victims receiving a satisfying redress through formalized systems of control. Rather, anarchism shows that crimes of unbridled force and repression are requisites for the rise and continuation of the machine itself—the state (Tifft and Sullivan 1980, chap. 2). Anarchism emphasizes not only that the greatest numbers and most egregious acts have been committed by the state, but also that the state has failed at controlling what it defines as crime.

Peacemaking criminology and abolitionism are central to anarchist responses (van Swaaningen 1997; Ward 1982, 120–25). Redefinitions of crime, rather than explications of current systems of law and domination, are fundamental. Furthermore, community responses to deviance (short of rationally organized systems of conflict resolution) are generally proposed as replacing faux community-based strategies such as community-based policing (Pepinsky 1993; Quinney and Pepinsky 1991; Sullivan 1980). Anarchism propagates the notion to actively live as "a counter friction to stop the machine" (Thoreau 1849/1957, 243).

Abolitionism offers much to the ongoing strategic debates. Originating in prison reform movements, abolitionism spread into criminology as a challenge to theoretical and practical ways of thinking about and responding to crime and justice. As a social strategy, abolitionism has gained ground in standing against crime and justice policies that support lengthy prison sentences, such as habitual offender statutes that in the end do not reduce crime (Kovandzic 2001). Abolitionism demands a rethinking of just what we mean by the widely used concepts—crime and punishment. Drawing from Nils Christie's (1981) writings of punishments as pain, abolitionism, like anarchism, suggests that crime, as a concept, serves no useful purpose. It also advocates a decentralized criminal justice system and redress through "real dialogue" as the means by which to envision conflict resolution. Abolitionism's position is that only in the most extreme cases should one's liberty be denied, and then for only a short time (van Swaaningen 1997). Abolitionism is presented as a means of addressing the crime and punishment problems through peaceful means. The desire—with anarchism, abolitionism, restorative, reintegrative, communitarian, and peacemaking criminology—is to move social life beyond violence inherent in state law and justice.

T. R. Young (1996a, 107) once suggested that the proper agenda for "affirmative criminology" is "a transition to a peaceable and praxical society." The implication is that criminology disassociate itself from current systems of pain infliction and advance less formal, reintegrative, peaceful, and communitarian strategies (Cordella 1996). Young and others offer directions for crime control practices that diverge from recent policies. Justice within these new directions, and for those who teach and practice it, implies a continual searching for conditions, whatever they may be, that promote cooperation and that allow parties—both those designated criminal and victim— to realize their human potential (or species being). To do otherwise disallows participation and denies human rights. Harm–reduction strategies are also central to progressive crime control (Nadelmann 2004). Humanely and pragmatically addressing the war on drugs, guaranteeing civil liberties to those accused, and extending all the rights to those offended are important to harm reduction. Thoughtful implementation of reducing criminal opportunities requires an ethical and humane commitment to human rights, people's freedom of movement, and public use of public space (see, e.g., Wilcox et al. 2003, chap. 9; Ferrell 2001, chap. 6).

Foreign to our current state-centered responses to crime, these more peaceful strategies are holistic; they hold offenders accountable and engage the various participants while encouraging a reintegrative shaming within supportive communities. They are worthy of consideration and honest debate for addressing predatory crime and the conditions under which it is produced.

REFERENCES

Akers, Ronald L. 1998. *Social Learning and Social Structure: A General Theory of Crime and Deviance*. Boston: Northeastern University Press.

———. 1991. *Drugs, Alcohol and Society*. Belmont, CA: Wadsworth.

———. 1985. *Deviant Behavior: A Social Learning Approach*. 3rd ed. Belmont, CA: Wadsworth.

Akerstrom, Malin. 1993. "Looking at the squares: Comparisons with the square johns." Pp. 23–31 in *In Their Own Words: Criminals on Crime*, ed. Paul Cromwell. Los Angeles: Roxbury.

———. 1985. *Crooks and Squares*. New Brunswick, NJ: Transaction.

Austin, James, and John Irwin. 2001. *It's About Time: America's Imprisonment Binge*. Belmont, CA: Wadsworth.

Barak, Gregg. 1998. *Integrating Criminologies*. Boston: Allyn and Bacon.

———. 1988. "Newsmaking criminology: Reflections on the media, intellectuals, and crime." *Justice Quarterly* 5 (4): 565–87.

Becker, Howard. 1963. *Outsiders*. New York: Free Press.

Bennett, Trevor, and Richard Wright. 1984. *Burglars on Burglary: Prevention and the Offender*. Hampshire, UK: Gower.

Benson, Michael L. 1985. "Denying the guilty mind: Accounting for involvement in a white-collar crime." *Criminology* 23 (4): 589–99.

Benson, Michael L., and Francis T. Cullen. 1998. *Combating Corporate Crime*. Boston: Northeastern University Press.

Berger, Peter L. 1963. *Invitation to Sociology*. New York: Anchor.

Bernasco, Wim, and Floor Luykx. 2003. "Effects of attractiveness, opportunity, and accessibility to burglars on residential burglary rates of urban neighborhoods." *Criminology* 41 (3): 981–1001.

Bernburg, Jon G., and Thorolfur Thorlindsson. 2001. "Routine activities in social context: A closer look at the role of opportunity in deviant behavior." *Justice Quarterly* 18 (3): 543–67.

Black, Donald. 1984. *Toward a General Theory of Social Control.* New York: Academic Press.

Blumstein, Alfred. 1986. *Criminal Careers and Career Criminals.* Vol. 1. Washington, DC: National Academy Press.

Bourdieu, Pierre. 1993. *Sociology in Question.* Thousand Oaks, CA: Sage.

Bowker, Lee H. 1998. *Masculinities and Violence.* Thousand Oaks, CA: Sage.

Braithwaite, John. 1994. *Crime, Shame and Reintegration.* Cambridge: Cambridge University Press.

Braithwaite, John, and Kathleen Daly. 1994. "Masculinities, violence and communitarian control." Pp. 189–213 in *Just Boys Doing Business?: Men, Masculinities and Crime,* ed. Tim Newburn and Elizabeth A. Stanko. London: Routledge.

Braithwaite, John, and Philip Pettit. 1990. *Not Just Deserts.* Oxford: Clarendon.

Brownfield, David. 1996. "The drugs and crime connection and offense specialization." Pp. 125–56 in *Criminological Controversies,* ed. John Hagan, A. R. Gillis, and David Brownfield. Boulder, CO: Westview.

Burgess, Robert L., and Ronald L. Akers. 1966. "A differential association-reinforcement theory of criminal behavior." *Social Problems* 14: 128–47.

Bursik, Robert J. 1988. "Social disorganization and theories of crime and delinquency: Problems and prospects." *Criminology* 26: 519–51.

Bursik, Robert J., and Harold G. Grasmick. 1993. *Neighborhoods and Crime.* New York: Lexington Books.

Carlson, Susan M., and Raymond J. Michalowski. 1997. "Crime, unemployment, and social structures of accumulation: An inquiry into historical contingency." *Justice Quarterly* 14 (2): 209–39.

Chambliss, William J. 1987. "I wish I didn't know now what I didn't know then." *The Criminologist* 12: 6.

———. 1973. "The saints and the roughnecks." *Society* 11: 24–31.

Chesney-Lind, Meda, and Vickie V. Paramore. 2001. "Are girls getting more violent?" *Journal of Contemporary Criminal Justice* 17 (2): 142–66.

Chilton, Roland, and Jim Galvin. 1985. "Race, crime, and criminal justice." *Crime and Delinquency* 31: 3–14.

Christie, Nils. 1993. *Crime Control as Industry.* London: Routledge.

———. 1981. *Limits to Pain.* Oslo: Universitetsforlaget.

Christie, Stuart. 1980. "Publisher's foreword." Pp. vii–xiii in *The Struggle to Be Human,* Larry Tifft and Dennis Sullivan. Mt. Pleasant, MI: Cienfuegos.

Cloward, Richard A., and Lloyd Ohlin. 1960. *Delinquency and Opportunity.* New York: Free Press.

Cohen, Stanley. 1993. "Human rights and crimes of the state: The culture of denial." *Australian and New Zealand Journal of Criminology* 26 (July): 97–115.

———. 1988. *Against Criminology.* New Brunswick, NJ: Transaction.

Coleman, James W. 1985. *The Criminal Elite.* New York: St. Martin's.

Cordella, Peter. 1996. "A communitarian theory of social order." Pp. 379–92 in *Readings in Contemporary Criminological Theory,* ed. Peter Cordella and Larry Siegel. Boston: Northeastern University Press.

Correctional education facts. 2004. *National Institute for Literacy* (September): www.nifl.gov/nifl/facts/correctional.

Cromwell, Paul F., James N. Olson, and D'Aunn Wester Avary. 1991. *Breaking and Entering: An Ethnographic Analysis of Burglary.* Thousand Oaks, CA: Sage.

Cullen, Francis T. 2005. "The twelve people who saved rehabilitation: How the science of criminology made a difference." *Criminology* 43 (1): 1–42.

Cullen, Francis T., and John P. Wright. 2004. "Employment, peers, and life-course transitions." *Justice Quarterly* 21 (1): 183–205.

Currie, Elliott. 1997. "Market society and market disorder." Pp. 37–42 in *Thinking Critically about Crime*, ed. Brian D. MacLean and Dragan Miovanovic. Vancouver: Collective Press.

———. 1996. "Missing pieces: Notes on crime, poverty, and social policy." *Critical Criminology* 7 (1): 37–52.

———. 1991. "The politics of crime: The American experience." Pp. 33–47 in *The Politics of Crime Control*, ed. Kevin Stenson and David Cowell. London: Sage.

———. 1985. *Confronting Crime: An American Challenge.* New York: Pantheon.

DeKeseredy, Walter S., Shahid Alvi, Martin D. Schwartz, and E. Andreas Tomaszewski. 2003. *Under Siege: Poverty and Crime in a Public Housing Community.* Lanham, MD: Lexington Books.

DeKeseredy, Walter S., Brian D. MacLean, and Martin D. Schwartz. 1997. "Thinking critically about left realism." Pp. 19–27 in *Thinking Critically about Crime*, ed. Brian D. MacLean and Dragan Milovanovic. Vancouver: Collective Press.

DeKeseredy, Walter S., and Martin D. Schwartz. 1996a. *Contemporary Criminology.* Belmont, CA: Wadsworth.

———. 1996b. "British and U.S. Left realism: A critical comparison." Pp. 305–18 in *Readings in Contemporary Criminological Theory*, ed. Peter Cordella and Larry Siegel. Boston: Northeastern University.

DeLisi, Matt. 2001. "Scaling archetypal criminals." *American Journal of Criminal Justice* 26 (1): 77–92.

Denton, John. 1990. *Society and the Official World.* Dix Hills, NY: General Hall.

DiMascio, William M. 1995. *Seeking Justice: Crime and Punishment in America.* New York: Edna McConnell Clark Foundation.

Dudley, Kathryn M. 1994. *The End of the Line.* Chicago: University of Chicago Press.

Durkheim, Emile. 1897/1951. *Suicide: A Study in Sociology.* New York: Free Press.

Farabee, David, Vandana Joshi, and M. Douglas Anglin. 2001. "Addiction careers and criminal specialization." *Crime and Delinquency* 47 (2): 196–220.

Farrington, David P. 2003. "Developmental and life-course criminology: Key theoretical and empirical issues." *Criminology* 41 (2): 221–55.

———. 1986. "Age and crime." Pp. 189–250 in *Crime and Justice* (Vol. 7), ed. Michael Tonry and Norval Morris. Chicago: University of Chicago Press.

Fattah, Ezzat A. 1997. "Toward a victim policy aimed at healing, not suffering." Pp. 257–72 in *Victims of Crime* (2nd ed.), ed. Robert C. Davis, Arthur J. Lurigio, and Wesley G. Skogan. Thousand Oaks, CA: Sage.

Federal Bureau of Prisons. 2004. Quick Facts, www.bop.gov.

Feeney, Floyd. 1986. "Robbers as decision-makers." Pp. 53–71 in *The Reasoning Criminal: Rational Choice Perspectives on Offending*, ed. Derek B. Cornish and Ronald V. Clarke. New York: Springer-Verlag.

Felson, Marcus. 1994. *Crime and Everyday Life*. Thousand Oaks, CA: Pine Forge.

Ferrell, Jeff. 2001. *Tearing Down the Streets*. New York: Palgrave.

———. 1997. "Against the law: Anarchist criminology." Pp. 146–54 in *Thinking Critically about Crime*, ed. Brian D. MacLean and Dragan Milovanovic. Vancouver: Collective Press.

———. 1995. "Style matters: Criminal identity and social control." Pp. 169–89 in *Cultural Criminology*, ed. Jeff Ferrell and Clinton R. Sanders. Boston: Northeastern University Press.

———. 1993. *Crimes of Style*. New York: Garland.

———. 1992. "Making sense of Crime: A review essay on Jack Katz's *Seductions of Crime*." *Social Justice* 19 (3): 110–23.

Ferrell, Jeff, and Clinton R. Sanders. 1995. *Cultural Criminology*. Boston: Northeastern University Press.

Frazier, Charles E., and Thomas Meisenhelder. 1985. "Criminality and emotional ambivalence: Exploratory notes on an overlooked dimension." *Qualitative Sociology* 8: 266–84.

Gadd, David, and Stephen Farrall. 2004. "Criminal careers, desistance and subjectivity: Interpreting men's narratives of change." *Theoretical Criminology* 8 (2): 123–56.

Gans, Herbert J. 1995. *The War against the Poor*. New York: Basic.

Garland, David. 1995. "Penal modernism and postmodernism." Pp. 181–209 in *Punishment and Social Control*, ed. Thomas G. Blomberg and Stanley Cohen. New York: Aldine de Gruyter.

Gentry, Cynthia. 1995. "Crime control through drug control." Pp. 477–92 in *Criminology* (2nd ed.), ed. Joseph F. Sheley. Belmont, CA: Wadsworth.

Glueck, Sheldon, and Eleanor Glueck. 1968. *Delinquents and Nondelinquents in Perspective*. Cambridge, MA: Harvard University Press.

Goldman, Emma. 1969. *Anarchism and Other Essays*. New York: Dover.

Goode, Erich, and Nachman Ben-Yehuda. 1994. *Moral Panics: The Social Construction of Deviance*. Cambridge: Blackwell.

Gottfredson, Michael, and Travis Hirschi. 1990. *A General Theory of Crime*. Stanford, CA: Stanford University Press.

Gusfield, Joseph R. 1963. *Symbolic Crusade*. Urbana: University of Illinois Press.

Hagan, John. 1997. "Defiance and despair: Subcultural and structural linkages between delinquency and despair in the life course." *Social Forces* 76 (1): 119–34.

———. 1996. "The class and crime controversy." Pp. 1–15 in *Criminological Controversies*, ed. John Hagan, A. R. Gills, and David Brownfield. Boulder, CO: Westview.

———. 1994. *Crime and Disrepute*. Thousand Oaks, CA: Pine Forge.

———. 1992. "The poverty of a classless criminology." *Criminology* 30 (1): 1–19.

Hagan, John, and Ruth D. Peterson. 1995. "Criminal inequality in America." Pp. 14–36 in *Crime and Inequality*, ed. John Hagan and Ruth D. Peterson. Stanford, CA: Stanford University.

Hagedorn, John. 1988. *People and Folks*. Chicago: Lake View Press.

Hall, Jerome. 1952. *Theft, Law and Society*. Indianapolis: Bobbs-Merrill.

Hamm, Mark S. 1997. *Apocalypse in Oklahoma*. Boston: Northeastern University Press.

———. 1993. *American Skinheads*. Westport, CT: Praeger.

Harrington, Michael. 1962. *The Other America*. New York: Macmillan.

Harrison, Paige M., and Jennifer C. Karberg. 2004. "Prison and jail inmates." *Bureau of Justice Statistics* (May). Washington, DC: U.S. Department of Justice.

Henry, Stuart. 1978. *The Hidden Economy*. London: Martin Robertson.

Hochstetler, Andy. 2001. "Opportunities and decisions: Interactional Dynamics in Robbery and Burglary Groups." *Criminology* 39 (3): 737–63.

Honaker, David. 1990. *Aging, Peers, and the Propensity for Crime: A Contextual Analysis of Criminal Decision Making* (Unpublished Master's Thesis). Knoxville: University of Tennessee.

hooks, bell. 2000. *Where We Stand: Class Matters*. Philadelphia: Taylor and Francis.

Horowitz, Irving. 1964. *The Anarchists*. New York: Bell.

Irwin, John. 1980. *Prisons in Turmoil*. Boston: Little, Brown.

———. 1970. *The Felon*. Englewood Cliffs, NJ: Prentice-Hall.

Jacobs, Bruce A. 2000. *Robbing Drug Dealers*. New York: Aldine de Gruyter.

Jacobs, Bruce A., and Richard Wright. 1999. "Stick-up, street culture, and offender motivation." *Criminology* 37 (1): 149–73.

Jansen, Robert W., and Peter J. Van Koppen. 1999. "The time to rob: Variations in time of number of commercial robberies." *Journal of Research in Crime and Delinquency* 36 (1): 7–29.

Jefferson, Tony. 1994. "Theorising masculine subjectivity." Pp. 10–31 in *Just Boys Doing Business?: Men, Masculinities and Crime*, ed. Tim Newburn and Elizabeth A. Stanko. London: Routledge.

Karmen, Andrew. 1996. *Crime Victims*. 3rd ed. Belmont, CA: Wadsworth.

Katz, Jack. 1988. *Seductions of Crime: Moral and Sensual Attractions in Doing Evil*. New York: Basic.

Kinsey, Richard, John Lea, and Jock Young. 1986. *Losing the Fight against Crime*. Oxford: Basil Blackwell.

Klockars, Carl B. 1974. *The Professional Fence*. New York: Macmillan.

Kovandzic, Tomislav V. 2001. "The impact of Florida's habitual offender law on crime." *Criminology* 39 (1): 179–203.

Kropotkin, Peter. 1898/1992. *Words of a Rebel*. Montreal: Black Rose Books.

Laub, John H. 1997. "Patterns of criminal victimization in the United States." Pp. 9–26 in *Victims of Crime* (2nd ed.), ed. Robert C. Davis, Arthur J. Lurigio, and Wesley G. Skogan. Thousand Oaks, CA: Sage.

Laub, John H., and Robert J. Sampson. 2003. *Shared Beginnings, Divergent Lives: Delinquent Boys to Age 70*. Cambridge, MA: Harvard University Press.

Lea, John. 1992. "The analysis of crime." Pp. 69–94 in *Rethinking Criminology: The Realist Debate*, ed. Jock Young and Roger Matthews. London: Sage.

Lea, John, and Jock Young. 1984. *What Is to Be Done about Law and Order?* Hammondsworth: Penguin.

Levi, Michael. 1994. "Masculinities and white-collar crime." Pp. 234–52 in *Just Boys Doing Business?: Men, Masculinities and Crime*, ed. Tim Newburn and Elizabeth A. Stanko. London: Routledge.

Lindesmith, Alfred R. 1968. *Addiction and Opiates*. Chicago: Aldine.

Lowman, John. 1992. "Rediscovering crime." Pp. 141–60 in *Rethinking Criminology: The Realist Debate*, ed. Jock Young and Roger Matthews. London: Sage.

Lowman, John, and Brian MacLean. 1992. "Introduction: Left realism, crime control, and policing in the 1990s." Pp. 3–29 in *Realist Criminology*, ed. John Lowman and Brian MacLean. Toronto: University of Toronto.

Luckenbill, David F. 1981. "Generating compliance: The case of robbery." *Urban Life* 10: 25–46.

———. 1977. "Criminal homicide as a situated transaction." *Social Problems* 25 (2): 176–86.

Lynch, Michael J., and W. Byron Groves. 1989. *A Primer in Radical Criminology*. New York: Harrow and Heston.

Lyng, Stephen. 1998. "Dangerous Methods: Risk taking and the research process." Pp. 221–51 in *Ethnography at the Edge*, ed. Jeff Ferrell and Mark S. Hamm. Boston: Northeastern University Press.

———. 1990. "Edgework: A social psychological analysis of voluntary risk taking." *American Journal of Sociology* 95 (4): 851–86.

Mangum, Garth L., Stephen L. Mangum, and Andrew W. Sum. 2003. *The Persistence of Poverty in the United States*. Baltimore: Johns Hopkins University Press.

Manning, Peter K. 1997. *Police Work*. 2nd ed. Prospect Heights, IL: Waveland.

Marks, Carole. 1991. "The urban underclass." *Annual Review of Sociology* 17: 445–66.

Martin, Dannie M., and Peter Y. Sussman. 1993. *Committing Journalism: The Prison Writings of Red Hog*. New York: Norton.

Marx, Karl. 1981. "On capital punishment." Pp. 55–56 in *Crime and Capitalism*, ed. David F. Greenberg. Palo Alto, CA: Mayfield.

———. 1934. *The Class Struggles in France*. New York: International Publishers.

Marx, Karl, and Frederick Engels. 1948. *The Communist Manifesto*. New York: International Publishers.

Massey, Douglas S., and Nancy A. Denton. 1993. *American Apartheid: Segregation and the Making of the Underclass*. Boston, MA: Harvard University Press.

Matthews, Roger, and Jock Young. 1992. "Reflections on realism." Pp. 1–23 in *Rethinking Criminology: The Realist Debate*, ed. Jock Young and Roger Matthews. London: Sage.

Matza, David, and Gresham Sykes. 1961. "Juvenile delinquency and subterranean values." *American Sociological Review* 26: 712–20.

McKeganey, Neil P. 1996. *Sex Work on the Streets*. Philadelphia: Open University Press.

McShane, Marilyn D., and Frank P. Williams III. 1992. "Radical victimology: A critique of the concept of victim in traditional victimology." *Crime and Delinquency* 38 (2): 258–71.

Merton, Robert K. 1957. *Social Theory and Social Structure*. New York: Free Press.

Messerschmidt, James W. 1993. *Masculinities and Crime*. Lanham, MD: Rowman & Littlefield.

Messner, Steven F., and Richard Rosenfeld. 2001. *Crime and the American Dream*. Belmont, CA: Wadsworth.

Miethe, Terrance D., and Richard McCorkle. 1998. *Crime Profiles*. Los Angeles: Roxbury.

Miller, Walter B. 1958. "Lower class culture as a generating milieu of gang delinquency." *Journal of Social Issues* 14 (3): 5–19.

Mills, C. Wright. 1956. *The Power Elite*. Oxford: Oxford University Press.

More than three-quarters of prisoners had abused drugs in the past. 1999. Bureau of Justice Statistics. Washington, DC: U.S. Department of Justice (January 15).

Moore, Joan. 1991. *Going Down to the Barrio: Homeboys and Homegirls in Change*. Philadelphia: Temple University Press.

Mullins, Christopher W., and Richard Wright. 2003. "Gender, social networks, and residential burglary." *Criminology* 41 (3): 813–39.

Nadelmann, Ethan A. 2004. "Criminologists and punitive drug prohibition: To serve or to challenge?" *Criminology and Public Policy* 3 (3): 441–50.

National Institute of Justice. 1996. "1995 Drug Use Forecasting." Washington, DC: U.S. Department of Justice (June).

Nelken, David. 1994. "Reflexive criminology?" Pp. 7–42 in *The Futures of Criminology*, ed. David Nelken. Thousand Oaks, CA: Sage.

Newburn, Tim, and Elizabeth A. Stanko. 1994. *Just Boys Doing Business?: Men, Masculinities and Crime*. London: Routledge.

O'Hare, William P., and Kenneth M. Johnson. 2004. "Child poverty in rural America." *Reports on America* (March). Washington, DC: Population Reference Bureau.

Pakulski, Jan, and Malcolm Waters. 1996. *The Death of Class*. Thousand Oaks, CA: Sage.

Parks, Robert E., Ernest W. Burgess, and Roderick McKenzie. 1925. *The City*. Chicago: University of Chicago Press.

Paternoster, Raymond, and Leeann Iovanni. 1985. "The labeling perspective and delinquency: An elaboration of the theory and an assessment of the evidence." *Justice Quarterly* 6: 359–94.

Pepinsky, Hal. 1995. "Peacemaking Primer." *Peace and Conflict Studies* 2 (2): 32–53.

———. 1993. "What is crime? What is peace?: A commentary." *Journal of Criminal Justice Education* 4 (2): 391–94.

Peterson, George E., and Adele V. Harrell. 1992. "Inner-city isolation and opportunity." Pp. 1–26 in *Drugs, Crime, and Social Isolation*, ed. Adele V. Harrell and George E. Peterson. Washington, DC: Urban Institute.

Peterson, Mark A., Harriet B. Braiker, and Suzanne M. Polich. 1980. *Doing Crime: A Survey of California Prison Inmates*. Santa Monica, CA: Rand.

Piquero, Alex, and George F. Rengert. 1999. "Studying deterrence with active residential burglars." *Justice Quarterly* 16 (2): 451–71.

Pirsig, Robert M. 1974. *Zen and the Art of Motorcycle Maintenance*. New York: William Morrow.

Polsky, Ned. 1967. *Hustlers, Beats, and Others*. Chicago: Aldine.

Presdee, Mike. 2000. *Cultural Criminology and the Carnival of Crime*. London: Routledge.

Private interview. 1987/1988. Private interviews conducted by the author with repetitive property offenders. For greater details, see Kenneth D. Tunnell, *Choosing Crime: The Criminal Calculus of Property Offenders*. Chicago: Nelson–Hall, 1992, esp. chapter 2.

Quinn, Thomas. 1998. "Restorative justice: An interview with visiting fellow Thomas Quinn." *National Institute of Justice Journal* (March): 10–16. Washington, DC: National Institute of Justice.

Quinney, Richard. 1997. "Socialist humanism and critical/peacemaking criminology: The continuing project." Pp. 114–17 in *Thinking Critically about Crime*, ed. Brian D. MacLean and Dragan Milovanovic. Vancouver: Collective Press.

———. 1991a. "The way of peace: On crime, suffering, and service." Pp. 3–13 in *Criminology as Peacemaking*, ed. Richard Quinney and Harold Pepinsky. Bloomington: Indiana University Press.

———. 1991b. *Journey to a Far Place*. Philadelphia: Temple University Press.

———. 1977. *Class, State, and Crime*. New York: Longman.

Quinney, Richard, and Harold Pepinsky. 1991. *Criminology as Peacemaking*. Bloomington: Indiana University Press.

Rand, Alicia. 1987. "Transitional life events and desistance from delinquency and crime." Pp. 134–62 in *From Boy to Man, from Delinquency to Crime*, ed. Marvin Wolfgang, T. Thornberry, and R. Figlio. Chicago: University of Chicago.

Reiman, Jeffrey H. 1979. *The Rich Get Richer and the Poor Get Prison*. New York: John Wiley and Sons.

Rengert, George, and John Wasilchick. 1985. *Suburban Burglary*. Springfield, IL: Charles C. Thomas.

Reppetto, T. A. 1974. *Residential Crime*. Cambridge, MA: Ballinger.

Rodriguez, Nancy. 2005. "Restorative justice, communities, and delinquency: Whom do we reintegrate?" *Criminology and Public Policy* 4 (1): 103–30.

Rose, Dina R., and Todd R. Clear. 1998. "Incarceration, social capital, and crime: Implications for social disorganization theory." *Criminology* 36 (3): 441–79.

Ross, Jeffrey I. 2002. *The Dynamics of Political Crime*. Thousand Oaks, CA: Sage.

Rothman, David J. 1995. "More of the same: American criminal justice policies in the 1990s." Pp. 29–44 in *Punishment and Social Control*, ed. Thomas G. Blomberg and Stanley Cohen. New York: Aldine de Gruyter.

Ruggiero, Vincenzo. 1992. "Realist criminology: A critique." Pp. 123–40 in *Rethinking Criminology: The Realist Debate*, ed. Jock Young and Roger Matthews. London: Sage.

Sampson, Robert J., and W. B. Groves. 1989. "Community structure and crime: Testing social disorganization theory." *American Journal of Sociology* 94: 774–802.

Sampson, Robert J., and John H. Laub. 2003. "Life-course desisters? Trajectories of crime among delinquent boys followed to age 70." *Criminology* 41 (3): 555–92.

———. 1993. *Crime in the Making: Pathways and Turning Points through Life.* Cambridge, MA: Harvard University Press.

Sampson, Robert J., S. W. Raudenbush, and F. Earls. 1998. *Neighborhood Collective Efficacy: Does It Help Reduce Violence?* Washington, DC: U.S. Department of Justice.

Schwartz, Martin D., and David O. Friedrichs. 1994. "Postmodern thought and criminological discontent: New metaphors for understanding violence." *Criminology* 32 (2): 221–56.

Scraton, Phil, and Kathryn Chadwick. 1991. "The theoretical and political priorities of critical criminology." Pp. 161–85 in *The Politics of Crime Control,* ed. Kevin Stenson and David Cowell. London: Sage.

Selva, Lance H., and Robert M. Bohm. 1987. "A critical examination of the informalism experiment in the administration of justice." *Crime and Social Justice* 29: 43–57.

Sevigny, Eric L., and Jonathan P. Caulkins. 2004. "Kingpins or mules: An analysis of drug offenders incarcerated in federal and state prisons." *Criminology and Public Policy* 3 (3): 401–34.

Shaw, Clifford R., and Henry D. McKay. 1942. *Juvenile Delinquency and Urban Areas.* Chicago: University of Chicago Press.

Shover, Neal. 1996. *Great Pretenders.* Boulder, CO: Westview.

Skocpol, Theda. 1979. *States and Social Revolutions.* Cambridge: Cambridge University Press.

———. 1976. "Explaining revolutions: In quest of a social-structural approach." Pp. 155–75 in *The Uses of Controversy in Sociology,* ed. Lewis Coser and Otto Larson. New York: Free Press.

Spitzer, Steven. 1975. "Toward a Marxian theory of deviance." *Social Problems* 22: 638–51.

Steffensmeier, Darrell, and Emilie Allan. 1995. "Criminal behavior: Gender and age." Pp. 83–113 in *Criminology* (2nd ed.), ed. Joseph F. Sheley. Belmont, CA: Wadsworth.

Steffensmeier, Darrell, and Miles D. Harper. 1999. "Making sense of recent U.S. crime trends, 1980 to 1996/1998: Age composition effects and other explanations." *Journal of Research in Crime and Delinquency* 36 (3): 235–74.

Steffensmeier, Darrell J., and Robert M. Terry. 1986. "Institutional sexism in the underworld: A view from the inside." *Sociological Inquiry* 56: 304–23.

Stein, Michael C., and George J. McCall. 1994. "Home ranges and daily rounds: Uncovering community among urban nomads." *Research in Community Sociology,* Supplement 1: 77–94.

Stenson, Kevin. 1991. "Making sense of crime control." Pp. 1–32 in *The Politics of Crime Control,* ed. Kevin Stenson and David Cowell. London: Sage.

Sullivan, Dennis. 1980. *The Mask of Love.* Port Washington, NY: Kennikat Press.

Sullivan, Dennis, Peter Sanzen, and Kathryn Callaghan. 1987. "The teaching and studying of justice: Fostering the unspeakable vision of cooperation." *Crime and Social Justice* 29: 128–35.

Sullivan, Mercer. 1989. *Getting Paid: Youth Crime and Work in the Inner City*. Ithaca, NY: Cornell.

Sutherland, Edwin H. 1949. *White Collar Crime*. New York: Dryden.

Svennson, Robert. 2002. "Strategic offences in the criminal career context." *British Journal of Criminology* 42 (2): 395–411.

Thompson, Hunter S. 1965/1990. "Midnight on the coast highway." Pp. 110–11 in *Songs of the Doomed: Gonzo Papers, Volume 3*. New York: Pocket.

———. 1967. *Hell's Angels: A Strange and Terrible Saga*. New York: Random House.

Thoreau, Henry D. 1849/1957. *Civil Disobedience*. Boston: Houghton Mifflin.

Tifft, Larry, and Dennis Sullivan. 1980. *The Struggle to be Human: Crime, Criminology and Anarchism*. Mt. Pleasant, MI: Cienfuegos.

Tittle, Charles R. 1995. *Control Balance*. Boulder, CO: Westview.

Traugott, Mark. 1985. *Armies of the Poor*. Princeton, NJ: Princeton University Press.

Tunnell, Kenneth D. 2004. *Pissing on Demand: Workplace Drug Testing and the Rise of the Detox Industry*. New York: New York University Press.

———. 1998. "The politics of teaching sociologies of crime." *Free Inquiry in Creative Sociology* 26 (2): 145–51.

———. 1995. "Silence of the left: Reflections on critical criminology and criminologists." *Social Justice* 22 (1): 89–101.

———. 1992. *Choosing Crime: The Criminal Calculus of Property Offenders*. Chicago: Nelson–Hall.

———. 1990. "Property criminals as the lumpen proletariat: A serendipitous finding." *Nature, Society and Thought* 3 (1): 39–55.

Tunnell, Kenneth D., and Terry C. Cox. 1995. "Applying a subculture of violence thesis to an ongoing criminal lifestyle." *Deviant Behavior* 16 (4): 373–89.

Useem, Michael. 1984. *The Inner Circle*. Oxford: Oxford University Press.

van Swaaningen, Rene. 1997. "Abolitionism: An alternative vision of justice." Pp. 139–45 in *Thinking Critically about Crime*, ed. Brian D. MacLean and Dragan Milovanovic. Vancouver: Collective Press.

Vold, George B., Thomas J. Bernard, and Jeffrey B. Snipes. 2002. *Theoretical Criminology*. 5th ed. New York: Oxford University Press.

Walklate, Sandra. 1992. "Researching victims of crime: Critical victimology." Pp. 285–302 in *Realist Criminology*, ed. John Lowman and Brian MacLean. Toronto: University of Toronto.

Walliman, Isidor, Howard Rosenbaum, Nicholas Tatis, and George Zito. 1980. "Misreading Weber: The concept of 'macht.'" *Sociology* 14: 261–75.

Walters, Glen D. 1994. *Drugs and Crime in Lifestyle Perspective*. Thousand Oaks, CA: Sage.

Ward, Colin. 1982. *Anarchy in Action*. London: Freedom Press.

Warner, Barbara D. 1997. "Community characteristics and the recording of crime: Police recording of citizens' complaints of burglary and assault." *Justice Quarterly* 14 (4): 631–49.

Weber, Max. 1968. *Economy and Society (Volume 1)*. New York: Bedminster.

———. 1946. *Essays in Sociology*, ed. and trans. H. H. Gerth and C. W. Mills. New York: Oxford University Press.

Weisheit, Ralph A., David N. Falcone, and L. Edward Wells. 1999. *Crime and Policing in Rural and Small-Town America*. 2nd ed. Prospect Heights, IL: Waveland.

Williams, Terry C., and William Kornblum. 1985. *Growing Up Poor*. Lexington, MA: Lexington Books.

Wilcox, Pamela, Kenneth C. Land, and Scott A. Hunt. 2003. *Criminal Circumstance*. New York: Aldine de Gruyter.

Wilson, James Q. 1968. *Varieties of Police Behavior*. Cambridge, MA: Harvard University Press.

Wilson, William J. 1997. *When Work Disappears*. New York: Random House.

———. 1987. *The Truly Disadvantaged*. Chicago: University of Chicago Press.

Wolfgang, Marvin E., Terence P. Thornberry, and Robert M. Figlio. 1987. *From Boy to Man, From Delinquency to Crime*. Chicago: University of Chicago Press.

Wolfgang, Marvin E., Robert Figlio, and Thorsten Sellin. 1972. *Delinquency in a Birth Cohort*. Chicago: University of Chicago Press.

Wright, Erik O. 1997. *Class Counts*. Cambridge: Cambridge University Press.

———. 1985. *Classes*. London: Verso.

———. 1973. *The Politics of Punishment: A Critical Analysis of Prisons in America*. New York: Harper and Row.

Wright, Kevin N. 1985. *The Great American Crime Myth*. New York: Praeger.

Wright, Richard T., and Scott Decker. 1997. *Armed Robbers in Action*. Boston: Northeastern University Press.

———. 1994. *Burglars on the Job*. Boston: Northeastern University Press.

Wright, Richard T., S. H. Decker, A. K. Redfern, and D. L. Smith. 1992. "A snowball's chance in hell: Doing field research with residential burglars." *Journal of Research in Crime and Delinquency* 29 (2): 148–61.

Young, Jock. 1999. *The Exclusive Society*. Thousand Oaks, CA: Sage.

———. 1997. "Left realism: The basics." Pp. 28–36 in *Thinking Critically about Crime*, ed. Brian D. MacLean and Dragan Milovanovic. Vancouver: Collective Press.

———. 1992a. "Ten points of realism." Pp. 24–68 in *Rethinking Criminology: The Realist Debate*, ed. Jock Young and Roger Matthews. London: Sage.

———. 1992b. "Realist research as a basis for local criminal justice policy." Pp. 33–72 in *Realist Criminology*, ed. John Lowman and Brian MacLean. Toronto: University of Toronto.

———. 1991. "Left realism and the priorities of crime control." Pp. 146–60 in *The Politics of Crime Control*, ed. Kevin Stenson and David Cowell. London: Sage.

Young, T. R. 1996a. "Beyond crime and punishment." *Critical Criminology* 7 (1): 107–20.

———. 1996b. "Beyond crime and punishment: Democratic proposals for social justice." *Critical Criminology* 7 (2): 92–107.

INDEX

ABOUT THE AUTHOR

Kenneth D. Tunnell is a professor at Eastern Kentucky University. His previous books include *Choosing Crime, Political Crime in Contemporary America*, and *Pissing on Demand: Workplace Drug Testing and the Rise of the Detox Industry*. His articles have appeared in journals such as *Justice Quarterly, Deviant Behavior, Qualitative Sociology*, and the *Journal of Popular Culture*.